Catholicism
peter stanford

Launched in 1938, the **teach yourself** series grew rapidly in response to the world's wartime needs. Loved and trusted by over 50 million readers, the series has continued to respond to

lton Park, Abingdon, Oxon OX14
154. Lines are open 09.00–17.00,
e. Details about our titles and how

r Services, PO Box 545, Blacklick,
}-755-5645.

For Canada order enquiries: please contact McGraw-Hill Ryerson Ltd, 300 Water St, Whitby, Ontario L1N 9B6, Canada. Telephone: 905 430 5000. Fax: 905 430 5020.

Long renowned as the authoritative source for self-guided learning – with more than 50 million copies sold worldwide – the **teach yourself** series includes over 500 titles in the fields of languages, crafts, hobbies, business, computing and education.

British Library Cataloguing in Publication Data: a catalogue record for this title is available from the British Library.

Library of Congress Catalog Card Number: on file.

First published in UK 2008 by Hodder Education, part of Hachette Livre UK, 338 Euston Road, London, NW1 3BH.

First published in US 2008 by The McGraw-Hill Companies, Inc.

This edition published 2008.

The **teach yourself** name is a registered trade mark of Hodder Headline.

Copyright © 2008 Peter Stanford

Typeset by Transet Ltd., Coventry.
Printed in Great Britain for Hodder Education, an Hachette Livre UK Company, 338 Euston Road, London NW1 3BH, by CPI Cox and Wyman Ltd, Reading, Berkshire, RG1 8EX.

The publisher has used its best endeavours to ensure that the URLs for external websites referred to in this book are correct and active at the time of going to press. However, the publisher and the author have no responsibility for the websites and can make no guarantee that a site will remain live or that the content will remain relevant, decent or appropriate.

Hachette Livre UK's policy is to use papers that are natural, renewable and recyclable products and made from wood grown in sustainable forests. The logging and manufacturing processes are expected to conform to the environmental regulations of the country of origin.

Impression number	10 9 8 7 6 5 4 3 2 1
Year	2012 2011 2010 2009 2008

iii

contents

acknowledgements

To Catholics of my generation (born 1961), the idea that you could teach yourself Catholicism is, at first glance, a difficult one. We were brought up to believe that if you had any questions about your faith, you should turn to a priest. The world – including the Catholic one – has moved on from those times, but I have still found myself, in writing this, turning to priests and theologians for advice and guidance on key questions of doctrine. I would like to thank in particular Fathers Shaun Middleton, John Hemer and Stephen McBrearty for all their hard work in guiding me during the researching and writing of this book.

All biblical quotations are from the *New Jerusalem Bible*, published by Darton, Longman and Todd. Quotations from *The Catechism of the Catholic Church* come from the Revised Edition published by Geoffrey Chapman.

Peter Stanford

I thought long and hard when Peter asked me to write a few words as an introduction to this book. It was not that I was reticent about helping an old friend, or that I feared he might not be up to task of explaining Catholicism. It's just that I could think of so many people more qualified for the task than me.

I have been a practising Catholic all my life. It remains an important part of who I am. But I certainly would never consider myself an expert.

There is no doubt that this book is timely. Faith and religion, for good and not-so-good reasons, are very much back on the public agenda. This makes it more important than ever that discussions are based on the facts rather than fiction, which is, sadly, not always the case.

It is giving the facts in a fair and balanced way that has been Peter's goal with this book about Catholicism. He believes, as I do, that going back to the basics in this way will promote understanding and tolerance, and help, too, to highlight the fundamental and decent values which our great religions share.

I hope you find the book as informative and interesting as I did.

Cherie Booth QC
London, July 2008

part one

Catholicism – the basics

01

what is Catholicism?

In this chapter you will learn:
- about the key role of the Pope within Catholicism
- why Catholics are different from other Christians
- how today's Catholic Church regards other faiths.

The oldest institution in the Western world

The Catholic Church is the oldest institution in the Western world. Its history can be traced back over 2000 years to the life and times of Jesus Christ. From the tiny group of supporters (or disciples) who gathered around him during his lifetime, it developed rapidly after his death and resurrection. Initially Jesus's followers operated as a group within Judaism, based in Jerusalem, and preached about their crucified leader as the Jewish Messiah who rose from the dead and was the Son of God. However, under the influence of Saint Paul, who had not been amongst Jesus's circle, the message was widened to appeal to Jews and non-Jews (Gentiles) alike. Paul is known as the 'Apostle to the Gentiles' and his three missionary journeys, around the eastern Mediterranean and Middle East, prefaced the spread of Christianity as a distinctive Church throughout the Roman Empire.

For its first millennium, the Catholic Church was the only institution in the Christian world, though there were many practical and doctrinal disputes in that period amongst its leaders as to how best to follow Jesus. Thereafter, successive splits, schisms and divisions with Orthodox Christians in the East, and then with Lutherans, Protestants, Anglicans and many others in the West left Christianity divided. Catholicism, however, remains Christianity's largest single organization and arguably its most influential.

The scale of world Catholicism (taken from current Vatican statistics)

Number of Catholics worldwide: 1.2 billion
Catholics as a percentage of world population: 17 per cent
Most Catholics in one country: Brazil with 125 million Catholics
Highest percentage of Catholics in one country: The Vatican City State 100 per cent (out of just 850 residents)

Geographical spread of Catholicism (as percentage of total population):
The Americas: 50 per cent
Europe: 26 per cent
Africa: 13 per cent
Asia: 10 per cent
Oceania: 1 per cent

Growth rates in number of Catholics in past decade:
Africa: 150 per cent
Asia: 74 per cent
Oceania: 49 per cent
The Americas: 45 per cent
Europe: 5 per cent

An historical overview

The origins of Catholicism – and in particular of the role of the papacy at the head of the Church – are complex and will be examined in greater detail in subsequent chapters. However, in considering a Church that has defied all predictions of its demise and has endured for 2000 years, it is important at the outset to give a brief historical overview.

Saint Peter, Jesus's chosen leader for his fledgling Church, worked after Christ's death with the other Apostles, and especially with Saint Paul, a Greek-speaking convert, to carry the new faith beyond Jerusalem and Judaism. In AD 64, both Peter and Paul were executed on the orders of the Roman Emperor, Nero. It is said that Peter was crucified upside down and that his body was buried on the spot in Rome where today stands the mother church of world Catholicism, the Basilica of St Peter's. In 1950 Pope Pius XII announced to the world that archaeologists had found evidence of Peter's tomb underneath the basilica.

It was only in the late second century, however, that Peter began to be described as the first Bishop of Rome and as Pope (from *papa*, the Latin for father). As the fledgling Church grew in size, despite fierce persecution from the Roman authorities, it started to imitate the hierarchical leadership model of the Roman Empire. Hence the development of the office of the Pope at the head of the Catholic Church and the role given to bishops as leaders of local communities of Christians. Eventually in 312 the Emperor Constantine attached Christianity's emblem to the banner of his troops and it became the official religion of the empire.

When the western part of that empire slowly crumbled in the fourth and fifth centuries, the papacy managed to retain its power and influence in the chaos that ensued. Under exceptional leaders like Pope Gregory the Great (590–604: in this book all dates given for Popes will signify their periods in office), it successfully evangelized the pagan forces that were destroying the Roman Empire and so laid the basis for a whole new Christian civilization in the West.

In the eleventh century there was a break with Christians in the East – the Orthodox – which was never subsequently mended. With the Renaissance of the fourteenth and fifteenth centuries, the dominance of papal, Catholic Christendom across Europe was undermined by social, economic and cultural factors. A German monk, Martin Luther, at the start of the sixteenth century, dealt a heavy blow to the authority of the Pope, setting up his own Church. His lead was followed by other Protestant reformers, but at the Council of Trent (1545–63), Catholicism regrouped as an instinctively traditional Church for most of the next four centuries.

The advent of Pope John XXIII (1958–63) unleashed a period of what he called *aggiornamento*, or 'opening a window on the world'. The Church's hostility to anything perceived as 'new' was ended and Catholicism was renewed and reinvigorated at the landmark Second Vatican Council (1962–5). Old prejudices against other Christian churches were replaced by a commitment to mutual exploration of common ground. Constructive engagement with the outside world blossomed with a high premium placed on social justice rather than older notions of charitable work.

This commitment to be part of the modern world found eloquent expression in the high profile involvement of John Paul II in the struggle to end Soviet communism's grip on his native Poland and Eastern Europe, which culminated in the fall of the Berlin Wall in 1989.

How are Catholics different from other Christians?

Other members of the wider Christian family share the same belief and roots in the life, teachings, death and resurrection of Jesus Christ, but the Catholic Church is unique in its claim that its head, the Pope, stands in a direct line back to Saint Peter, the one among Jesus's 12 Apostles, the gospels report, to whom the founder chose to entrust his followers.

Peter, a married fisherman on the Sea of Galilee, was originally known as Simon. However, Jesus gave him a new name – *Kephas* in Aramaic, the language he would have used, meaning 'rock'.

The Greek translation of this is rendered in English as Peter. 'You are Peter,' Jesus tells him in Chapter 16 of St Matthew's Gospel (an account of Jesus's life), 'and on this rock I will build my Church… I will give you the gates of the kingdom of heaven: whatever you bind on earth shall be considered bound in heaven.'

The 'Apostolic Succession' – the idea that Jesus's mandate to Peter has been passed on to each and every one of his 260 plus successors as Pope – lies at the very core of Catholicism. The Pope has supreme authority within the Church for interpreting Christ's teachings. This has been its custom from earliest times, but was given formal recognition in 1870 when it was declared that the Pope can, when he wishes, speak infallibly on matters of faith and morals. He cannot make mistakes, Catholicism teaches, because he is being guided by the Holy Spirit. Like other Christian faiths, Catholicism is Trinitarian, that is it believes that there are three persons in the One God, the Father, Jesus, his son, and the Holy Spirit.

But it is not only the paramount role of the Pope that marks out Catholicism. The Church's practice of the faith, especially its rigorous emphasis on the duty to attend the sacraments regularly and on questions of personal and public morality, also distinguish it from other Christian churches.

Catholicism prides itself, too, on standing apart from trends in broader society and defending what it describes as 'eternal truths'. It is said that its attitudes move not in months, years or even decades, but over the course of centuries. It says of itself that it has never compromised teachings handed down by Jesus Christ to the Apostles because it does not have the authority to override scripture. Therefore it cannot, for example, ordain women to its priesthood because Jesus did not choose women among his 12 original Apostles.

The claim never to change its stance on such 'God-made' teachings is, however, disputed. Catholic interpretation of some key passages in the four gospels has certainly altered over the centuries, as will be discussed in subsequent chapters. What is undeniably true, though, is that Catholicism has often found itself at odds with the mores and morality of the society in which it has operated from Renaissance times onwards. In recent times, for example, Pope John Paul II (1978–2005) was fond of remarking that Catholicism was 'a sign of contradiction' in an increasingly secular modern society.

Though many outside the Catholic Church use the term Roman Catholics to describe those who accept the *magisterium* – or supreme teaching authority – of the popes, based in the Vatican in Rome, many of those inside the Church refer to themselves simply as Catholics. This can occasionally lead to confusion. There are, for instance, those within Anglicanism who call themselves Catholic, imitating many features of Roman liturgy, but rejecting the supreme authority of the Pope.

The distinguishing features of Catholicism

1 **Its history:** Catholicism's survival and continuing success in attracting additional members globally after 2000 years gives it a certain identity and self-confidence. Some Church theologians see an organic growth over those two millennia, picturing Catholicism as a gigantic old tree, in a state of permanent development, shedding dead branches and poor fruit, as it matures towards an ultimate perfection.

2 **The role of the papacy:** Though it was not until 1870 that the Pope was declared infallible 'in matters of faith and morals', in practice the authority of the papacy has given a unique definition to Catholic teaching throughout the ages.

3 **Its priesthood:** The Catholic priesthood remains reserved, in all but a tiny handful of cases, to celibate men. The Church twins vocation to the priesthood with vocation to celibacy. Women remain excluded from the priesthood on the grounds of their gender.

4 **Its teachings:** The Catholic Church goes against current secular norms by teaching that divorce, masturbation, sex before and outside marriage, homosexuality and all artificial means of contraception are sinful. It will not sanction the use by its faithful of condoms, even if their intention is to prevent the spread of HIV/AIDS, on the grounds that they would prevent the transmission of life. Pro-life in the widest sense, Catholicism not only opposes abortion but also the death penalty, while it promotes access to better education, health care, employment and housing for the needy of the world.

5 **Its liturgy:** While Latin is no longer the standard language around the globe of the Catholic liturgy (its church services), the Church continues to stand apart from other Christian faiths in its insistence, as part of its belief in what is called transubstantiation, that at the moment of consecration,

during the celebration of the Eucharist (Holy Communion), Christ is present in the bread and wine in more than a symbolic way.

6 **Its practices:** The Catholic Church requires weekly mass attendance; encourages veneration of Jesus's mother, the Blessed Virgin Mary, and 'the company of saints'; strongly encourages prayers for the dead as a way of interceding on their behalf to speed their journey; and endorses claims of miraculous cures achieved either through the intercession of those individuals it has chosen posthumously to declare saints, or by attendance at one of a number of officially sanctioned shrines. While each of these practices is not unique to Catholicism, together they form a body of behaviour that distinguishes it from other Churches and which can, on occasion, cause controversy.

7 **The emphasis it places on the role of the Holy Spirit:** Catholicism, like other Christian churches, teaches of the Trinity, the three persons in One God, but it gives the Spirit certain distinctive roles: in enabling communication with Christ, in bestowing 'gifts of the Spirit' on believers, in promoting the unity of the Church and, even, in guiding the cardinal electors when they chose a new pope.

Attitude to other faiths

Once Christianity had expanded beyond its original Jewish base, it sought to play down its Jewish roots in order to form its own distinctive identity. This led to it being responsible, for many centuries, for encouraging the scapegoating of Jews, accusing them of deicide – killing the Son of God. In the aftermath of the Protestant Reformation of the sixteenth century, Catholicism also came to regard newer Christian Churches with great hostility.

However, these prejudices were definitively rejected at the Second Vatican Council. In the decades that have followed it, the Catholic Church has expended a great deal of energy on building better relationships with other faiths. One spectacular high point was the gathering Pope John Paul II hosted in the Italian city of Assisi in October 1986, when he stood in a circle with Anglicans, Buddhists, Hindus, Sikhs, Shintoists and African and Amerindian animists who passed around a pipe of peace. The event, John Paul said, 'has taught us anew to be aware of the common origin and the common destiny of humanity'.

Particular emphasis has been given to entering into dialogues with other mainstream Protestant Churches. This led, in the 1970s and 1980s, to hopes of an eventual Christian reunion. However, discussion has stalled over key doctrinal questions such as Eucharist, ministry and the papacy, where Catholic teaching and practice is at odds with that in its 'sister churches'. In spite of such substantial theological obstacles, much goodwill and practical co-operation now exists, especially at grass roots level, and is seen, for example, in Catholic participation in annual Weeks of Prayer for Christian Unity and in national pan-Christian Councils of Churches.

With other non-Christian faiths, there have also been great steps forward. The 1965 Second Vatican Council document, *Nostra Aetate*, repudiated the idea that Jews had been responsible for deicide when Jesus was crucified. 'The death of Christ is not to be attributed to an entire people then alive,' it states, 'and even less to a people today. Therefore, let priests be careful not to say anything, in catechetical instruction or in preaching, that might give rise to hatred or contempt of the Jews in the hearts of their hearers.' All forms of anti-Semitism were repudiated. With Islam, successive popes have worked to develop a relationship with Muslim leaders founded on mutual respect and tolerance of the practice of each other's faith.

However, at its core Catholicism teaches that the 'Church of Christ' subsists within the Catholic Church. Therefore, it, rather than other faiths, represents the best route to salvation and eternal life with God. It has never abandoned its demand that its faithful evangelize those they meet.

The tension between these core beliefs and Catholic efforts to promote inter-faith dialogue was highlighted in July 2007, when the Vatican's Congregation for the Doctrine of the Faith published a document which set out with uncomfortable clarity that other Christian denominations 'cannot be called churches in the proper sense', while Eastern Orthodoxy, perhaps the closest cousin to Catholicism in the wider Christian family, was labelled as 'wounded' because it does not accept the supreme authority of the Pope.

Conclusion

Though the modern Catholic Church sees itself as part of a wider Christian family, and maintains good relationships with other Churches and faiths at international, national and local level, it also retains a distinct and unchanging identity. This is based on its particular interpretations of the gospels, its own traditions and practices and – most obviously – in its loyalty to the Pope as the *magisterium* (teaching authority) of the Church. As both a focus of unity in a global Church, and as a final decision-maker on disputed questions of faith and morals, the papacy enjoys great power, while the activities and pronouncements of individual popes, on the world stage, inevitably serve to draw attention to Catholicism, often at the expense of the more collective leaderships of other faiths.

02

once a Catholic

In this chapter you will learn:
- how attitudes have changed recently within Catholicism
- about the importance of tradition
- about the place of Mary.

A changing Church

Notions of what it means to be a Catholic have changed radically within the last 50 years as both society and the Church have changed. Within the Church, there used to be a popular argument, when confronted with internal dissent, that being a Catholic was akin to joining a club. If you didn't agree with its rules, you should leave, rather than demand change or flout the laws. An element of that fierce loyalty still exists, but today priests and bishops accept – privately and often publicly – that they can no longer command their congregations to do what they are told. There is a more thoughtful attitude to faith and practice, still guided by a profound respect for the teaching authority of the Pope and his bishops, but no longer the sort of obedience once associated with Catholics. The Church has returned to its original understanding of the word obedience – namely to hear and therefore to understand and assent unless conscience dictates otherwise.

Outside the Church, once-popular stereotypes of Catholics have fallen by the wayside as the world has come to recognize the diversity of belief among Catholics. It used to be expected, for example, that Catholics would usually be members of large families because of their Church's prohibition on the use of artificial contraceptives. Yet today, in many of the parishes of the developed world countries, most families will have, at most, two or three children.

Likewise, Catholics have a reputation for being riven by guilt, especially over sex. It is an attitude, again in the popular mind, that has been instilled in impressionable young Catholics by their teachers, especially nuns. However, it is an outdated image. The number of nuns teaching in schools has fallen dramatically, while approaches to sex and sexuality have become more nuanced and more accepting of the reality of people's lives. Marriage remains an ideal, for instance, but is no longer seen simply as the correct forum for sexual activity but also as a covenant of life and love between two heterosexual adults.

Guilt is no more prevalent in a new generation of Catholics than in the wider world. Whether the stereotype was ever true is a matter of dispute, though the novels of Catholic writers such as Graham Greene, Edna O'Brien and David Lodge present a strong case for the proposition.

Was Jesus Catholic?

No, he was a Jew and the origins of Christianity are as a reform movement within Judaism. The Catholic Church believes that Jesus's mission was not only for Jews but for the whole world. His intention was therefore, according to Catholic teaching, to found a new church, close to but distinct from Judaism. This wish was carried through after Jesus's death when his message was taken to non-Jews or Gentiles.

The Catholic Church shares with other Christian churches the aspiration to model itself on Jesus. 'He is "the perfect man", who invites us to become his disciples and follow him,' states the 1993 official rulebook, *The Catechism of the Catholic Church*. 'In humbling himself, he has given us an example to imitate, through his prayer he draws us to pray, and by his poverty he calls on us to accept freely the privation and persecutions that may come our way.' Other Christian churches have a similar approach.

Catholicism, moreover, teaches that it is Jesus, not the Pope, who is actually head of the Church and that he continues to dwell on earth in the form of the Catholic Church, until his return in the Second Coming. Again this is not unique. One distinguishing factor in the Catholic position – compared with, for example, Evangelical or fundamentalist Christianity – is its view that salvation is not limited to those who attend the sacraments of the Catholic Church. Jesus is, Catholicism holds, 'the universal sacrament of salvation', and hence is available to all; whatever their creed and regardless of whether they are Catholics.

What do Catholics believe?

An older generation of Catholics will recall that they learnt their faith not principally through reading the Bible, but instead through instruction from their priests and nuns, through their Catholic schools, and through the Catholic liturgy. The origin of this oral approach to conveying the essentials of Catholic beliefs lies in times when the vast majority of the population was illiterate and therefore unable to read scripture. However, it endured in Catholicism long after increasing levels of literacy had permitted other Christian denominations a greater concentration on individual study of the Bible as a way of learning how to be a true follower of Jesus Christ.

Catholicism, by contrast, continued into the twentieth century to see it as the role of the priest to pass on the beliefs and practice of the faith to his congregation. The priest acted as a kind of intermediary between God and his people. Because humankind was regarded as essentially sinful, there was an obligation assumed by the clergy to guide the faithful away from wrongful interpretation of key Biblical ideas and from resulting sinful behaviour. Catholics were largely discouraged from individual biblical study and towards conformity with the traditional practices of their Church.

It was only in 1909 that Pope Pius X founded the Pontifical Biblical Institute in Rome to encourage critical study of the scriptures. So, in recent times, Catholicism has, in a real sense, returned to being a 'religion of the book' with a new emphasis placed on scriptural study by clergy and laity alike, albeit alongside the more usual stand-bys of papal pronouncements and official rulebooks such as the old *Penny Catechism* and its successor, the 1993 *Catechism of the Catholic Church*.

The place of tradition and prayer

One time-honoured route in Catholicism to instilling an instinctive understanding of the faith was through what was called 'liturgical prayer'. The Church aimed to distil the essence of Catholicism into the words of the prayers that make up the liturgy or Mass. By saying, for example, the Apostles' Creed, all necessary key doctrines were transmitted to and absorbed by the faithful through constant repetition of the words. This was an approach known in Church circles by the Latin phrase *Lex orandi, lex credendi*, which translates as 'the law of prayer is the law of belief'. In other words, what you say out loud in the liturgy is what you believe.

This ancient Christian principle dates back to the early centuries of the Church before there was an agreed canon of scriptural texts. It was only in the early fifth century that Saint Jerome produced his *Vulgate*, an officially sanctioned translation into Latin of those books of the Old and New Testament that the Catholic Church was willing to sanction as its Bible. Many previously revered texts were excluded. They are known today as the 'Apocrypha', from the Greek word for things that have been 'hidden away', and can tell a very different story of Jesus from the Authorized Version.

The 'liturgical prayer' approach was used throughout the Church's history to allow its leaders to place, above the views of individual believers, an officially sanctioned interpretation of the extracts from scriptures included in the cycles of readings to be used in the Mass. The result of this process of transmission is what is sometimes called the *depositum fidei* – 'the deposit of the faith' – a phrase that embraces both the Bible *and* the interpretation of it made through the magisterium of the Church down through the ages.

Catholicism places a greater emphasis than other Christian denominations on the force of its own traditions. If the Church has always regarded something as morally unacceptable, Catholicism's firm presumption will be that shifting attitudes in outside society are no reason to change its own mind.

But, as Pius X acknowledged in 1909, such a system was open to abuse and risked treating the scriptures as if they were straightforward, black and white documents. They are not, and they contain many passages open to a variety of interpretations which demand to be read in the context of their times. In the case of the New Testament, for example, passages may have been added to the original oral accounts of Jesus's life in order to depict him as fulfilling Old Testament prophecies.

Equally, the four gospels, the official version of Jesus's time on earth, were written between 30 and 100 years after his death by scribes who may not have been eyewitnesses to the events they purport to describe. They are also, in places, contradictory. Only two of the gospels, for instance, include an account of Jesus's birth in Bethlehem, and only Luke's gospel presents the traditional picture of the manger and stable.

It becomes yet more complicated because Jesus did not speak in the gospels specifically on many of the moral dilemmas that confront contemporary Christianity and over which Catholicism takes such a firm stand. For example, he makes no reference at all to homosexuality. So Catholicism has based its centuries-old teaching that homosexuality is 'a strong tendency towards an intrinsic moral evil', as the Vatican reiterated in a 1986 document, on a reading of the general tone of Jesus's remarks on sexual morality, as well as earlier precedents in the Old Testament, along with its own stated position down the ages. It can be difficult for Catholics to distinguish between what are sometimes called 'God-made' (i.e. scriptural) and 'man-made' (i.e. dictated by the traditional practice of the Church) teachings.

The role of Mary

The overlapping of tradition and scripture in Catholic belief and practice can be seen in the unique stress the Church places on Mary, the mother of Jesus. Catholicism holds that Mary plays a special role in humankind's salvation, intervening on our behalf with her son. Some Catholics would rate her even more highly. In 1997, 4.35 million signatures were collected for an appeal to declare her 'Co-Redemptrix, Mediatrix of All Graces and Advocate for the People'. Pope John Paul II rejected the notion, on the advice of a Vatican commission, but throughout his pontificate promoted Mary as the supreme example of a Catholic woman and of how women should live their lives. He even placed the letter M at a central point in his papal coat of arms.

Yet, she features briefly in the gospels' accounts and little of what has later been claimed for her by Catholicism has any basis in the Bible. This is something the Church freely acknowledges. 'What the Catholic faith believes about Mary is based on what it believes about Christ,' the *Catechism of the Catholic Church* states plainly. Since the Church believes that Jesus was at once both human and divine – son of God *and* a man – it follows that his mother must have been an exceptional human being. So in Matthew's and Luke's gospels – but not in Mark's or John's – it is told that Mary gave birth to Jesus without first having sexual intercourse. Jesus's birth was a virgin birth. Traditional Catholicism used to describe the actual delivery as 'like light passing through glass'.

If the Virgin Birth divides the gospel writers, Catholic teaching about the Immaculate Conception – the belief that Mary, unlike the rest of humankind, was born without the stain of original sin which was, for everyone else, a shared legacy since Adam and Eve's fall in the Garden of Eden – receives only an oblique endorsement from Luke. He describes how the Angel Gabriel, on coming down from heaven to tell Mary that she is to bear God's son (an event known in Christianity as the Annunciation), greets her as 'full of grace'. From this phrase, Church Fathers down the ages have developed the notion that Mary was, as the *Universal Catechism* puts it, 'wholly borne by God's grace'. It continues: 'Through the centuries the Church has become ever more aware that Mary, "full of grace" through God, was redeemed from the moment of her conception.' The doctrine – or official teaching – of the Immaculate Conception dates back to 1854.

There is no scriptural basis at all for the third principal claim that Catholicism makes on Mary's behalf – its teaching that she was assumed body and soul into heaven when her earthly life ended. For all others, Catholicism teaches that the body is discarded and only the soul endures. However, Mary was set apart from this in 1950 by Pope Pius XII, who in doing so exercised the power, acquired in 1870, for popes to speak infallibly in matters of faith and morals.

Though the idea of Mary's Assumption, body and soul, into heaven was unknown in the early Church, she has been exalted by leading theologians throughout Church history. Saint Irenæus, bishop of Lyon in France in the second century, for example, is sometimes called the first theologian 'of the Virgin Mother'. He made a parallel, still repeated in Catholicism to this day, between Eve and Mary, urging that, 'as the former was led astray by an angel's discourse to fly from God after transgressing his word, so the latter by an angel's discourse had the gospel preached unto her that she might bear God, obeying his word. And if the former had disobeyed God, yet the other was persuaded to obey God: that the Virgin Mary might become an advocate for the virgin Eve. And as mankind was bound unto death through a virgin, it is saved through a virgin; by the obedience of a virgin the disobedience of a virgin is compensated.'

How such polarized attitudes to Mary and Eve within Catholicism have shaped its attitudes to the role of women is a matter for later chapters. What is important to note here is that, although official declarations of doctrine concerning the Virgin Mary are of relatively recent provenance, devotion to her has been a distinctive feature of Catholicism throughout its history. There is, for example, the tradition of reported apparitions of the Virgin Mary on earth, in her role as an intermediary between God and his people. In 352 a Roman nobleman, John, and his childless wife were convinced that the Virgin Mary came to them and miraculously intervened on their behalf to allow them to become parents. The Virgin's sign had been a snowflake falling on one of the Seven Hills of Rome and so a church was built in memory of Our Lady of the Snows where today stands the Basilica of St Mary Major.

In 1061, a Saxon noblewoman, Richeldis de Faverches, reported that Mary transported her from Walsingham, Norfolk, back to her own home in Nazareth. As a result, Lady Richeldis subsequently built a shrine to the Virgin in Walsingham which became a major centre of pilgrimage, attracting kings, queens and scholars, until Henry VIII ordered its dissolution in 1537 during the English Reformation.

Popular sites of Marian devotion

1 **Lourdes**, located in south-western France where, Catholics believe, Mary appeared 18 times in all in 1858 to a 14-year-old local girl, Bernadette Soubirous. The Virgin made a fountain spring up in a grotto at the site of the apparition and its water is believed to have miraculous healing powers. The shrine was inaugurated in 1873 and is amongst the best-known sites of pilgrimage in Catholic Europe.

2 **Knock**, in County Mayo, is Ireland's national shrine. In 1879, a silent Mary, along with her husband Joseph and John the Evangelist, is reported to have appeared to 15 local people. In 1979, Pope John Paul II visited Knock during his tour of Ireland.

3 **Fatima**, where for six consecutive months in 1917, Mary is said to have appeared in a blinding light to three peasant children in Portugal. Others at the scene saw the sun dance. Mary urged the seers to do penance, say the Rosary and pray for the conversion of Russia from communism. She also imparted three secrets. The first two – a vision of hell and guidance on how to save souls in hell – were made public, but it was only in 2000 that the Vatican revealed the third secret, a vision of a Pope-like figure being struck down by assailants, taken to be a reference to the 1981 assassination attempt in St Peter's Square by a lone Turkish gunman on John Paul II who was a particular devotee of Our Lady of Fatima.

4 **Czestochowa**, in southern Poland, is home to the Jasna Gora Monastery which houses the Black Madonna. Catholic legend states that this painting of Mary was done by Luke, the gospel writer, on a tabletop from the home of Jesus and his parents. It was brought to Czestochowa in 1382 from Jerusalem and is reported to have saved the Poles from foreign invaders.

5 **Garabandal**, in north-west Spain, was visited by the Virgin Mary many times between 1961 and 1965 according to four young girls. She gave them messages that urged the world to purify its heart and forgive sins. Though many pilgrims travel to the small village, the Catholic Church has officially discounted the visions.

6 **Medjugorje,** in Hercegovina in the former Yugoslavia, has, since June 1981, witnessed apparitions of the Virgin Mary – the 'Gospa' in the local Croatian language – to six young people. Her message of daily prayer and Bible reading, fasting and attendance of the sacraments has attracted many pilgrims, but the Vatican has yet to decide whether to give the shrine official sanction.

How Catholicism operates

The reforming Second Vatican Council declared that there should no longer be a division in Catholicism between those who are ordained and those who are not. Henceforth, it promised, both clergy and laity would be equal partners as 'the people of God'. That equality was rooted in a 'shared priesthood' of all Catholics, received at Baptism, but lived out in many different ways. The phrase 'the people of God', one of the most potent in Catholicism, occurs in the key Council document, *Lumen Gentium*, approved in November 1964. (Church documents often have Latin titles. In the case of *Lumen Gentium*, it translates as 'The Light of Nations'.)

The second chapter of *Lumen Gentium* – designated as a 'Constitution for the Church' – is entitled 'People of God', but is followed by a section called 'The Church is Hierarchical', which explains the essential leadership role of the Pope, cardinals, archbishops, bishops and priests within the Catholic community. In practice Catholicism remains, in its structures and mindset, a highly centralized, global organization with believers organized into parishes which make up dioceses headed by bishops, who report to archbishops and then cardinals who in turn both elect popes and carry through the teaching of the men they have chosen to lead them.

The Catholic Church is emphatically not a democracy. While popes hold regular synods on key issues like the family, evangelization and the place of women, they are under no binding obligation to act on the views they hear expressed by the clerical and lay representatives from around the world who attend. Different popes interpret their teaching authority in a variety of ways. Among key concepts at the Second Vatican Council was that of collegiality – that groups of local bishops in a particular country could decide how best to act on issues in accordance with the overall principles of their Church, without seeking formal approval from the Vatican.

This practice was, however, eroded during the papacy of John Paul II who believed that too much local autonomy would destroy the unity of the Church. So, for example, when in 1983 America's bishops wanted to publish a teaching document on nuclear weapons, the Vatican insisted on seeing the text first and making substantial amendments.

Catholicism as a way of life

Approaches to Catholic education – both of children and of adults – have altered considerably, with a greater emphasis now placed on the positive imperatives of Catholic teaching, especially with regard to love of neighbour and wider social responsibility. Talk of sinfulness, especially with regard to sex, or of the Devil and hell, is, by contrast, muted in comparison with what was heard in the classroom and from the pulpit 50 years ago. Much effort has been made to ensure that those who fall short of Catholic ideals in their personal life (for example, those who divorce or have children out of wedlock) do not feel excluded from or rejected by the Church. This can cause tensions, especially when the reality of the warm welcome offered by parish communities to those whose lives do not conform to Church teaching is set alongside doctrinal statements from Church leaders reiterating the ideals that lie behind those teachings.

There are many people today, especially in the Western world, who describe themselves as lapsed or cultural Catholics, brought up in the faith, still attached to it in some ill-defined way, but no longer regular Mass-goers. One of the distinctive features of Catholicism appears to be the way in which even those who reject some or all of the teachings they received in their Catholic childhood retain an emotional and spiritual link with the Church ever after.

The Catholic way of life today is built around the parish, the home and, where they are available, Catholic schools. A key feature is the obligation to attend Mass on Sundays and on a small number of Holy Days of Obligation throughout the year.

Holy Days of Obligation

These are decided by local bishops, who can move their commemoration to the nearest Sunday, but often include:

- January 6, The Feast of the Epiphany, marking the arrival of the three kings at Jesus's birthplace.
- The Thursday of the sixth week after Easter, known as Ascension Thursday, when Jesus's ascent into heaven is recalled.
- June 29, the Feast of Saints Peter and Paul.
- August 15, the Assumption, when Jesus's mother was raised body and soul into heaven.
- November 1, All Saints' Day.

The sacramental life

The place of the seven sacraments is crucial in giving a structure to the Catholic way of life:

1 **Baptism** – welcoming infants into the family of the Church – usually takes place within the first six months after birth.

2 **The first reception of the sacrament of Reconciliation** – once known as Confession or Penance – comes when the child is aged between seven and nine and immediately precedes First Holy Communion.

3 **Holy Communion** – receiving the bread and wine of the Eucharist as the body and blood of Christ – is the most central of the sacraments and is often referred to as 'the Bread of Life'.

4 **Confirmation** – making an adult commitment before a bishop to the faith – usually comes in mid-teens.

5 **The sacrament of Marriage** – the partnership of the couple *and* God as the basis for family life – remains a foundation stone of the Catholic approach even though marriage has declined in popularity in western secular society.

6 **Ordination** – or Holy Orders – takes place when a man becomes a priest after completing an average of eight years of study.

7 **The Sacrament of the Anointing of the Sick** – formerly known as the Last Rites or Extreme Unction ('final anointing') – is administered by a priest to those who may be approaching death.

Is there a Catholic morality?

The Catholic Church, like all other religious bodies, has a body of teachings, many of which touch on principles of individual and societal moral conduct. It places particular emphasis on two areas: the first concerning what might loosely be called social justice, and the second on pro-life issues. With regard to the first issue, Catholicism, often through local bishops or development agencies like the worldwide Caritas Internationalis network, is prominent in tackling economic injustice, political oppression and the abuse of human rights.

Its social teaching is often called Catholicism's 'best kept secret' and is contained in celebrated papal documents such as *Rerum Novarum* ('Of New Things'), *Pacem in Terris* ('On Establishing Universal Peace') and *Populorum Progressio* ('On the Development of Peoples').

The first of these, released in 1891 by Pope Leo XIII, supported the foundation of trade unions, laid the basis for the Christian Democratic parties of Europe in the twentieth century and attacked the notion that 'the wealthy and the working men are intended by nature to live in mutual conflict'.

The second, published in 1963 by Pope John XXIII in the wake of the erection of the Berlin Wall and the Cuban Missile Crisis which had caused fears for the future of humankind, was addressed not just to Catholics but 'to all men of good will'. It rejected the arms race, urged negotiation and set out, on the basis of Christian teaching, a universal human right to 'bodily integrity and to the means which are suitable for the proper development of life'.

The third was an urgent and ringing appeal from Pope Paul VI in 1967, and addressed itself to the consequences of global economic inequality. 'The world is sick. The poor nations remain poor while the rich ones become still richer. The very life of poor nations, civil peace in developing countries and world peace itself are at stake.'

With regard the second area of particular emphasis – concerning pro-life issues – the Catholic Church has taken an outspoken stance against anything that it believes interferes with the transmission of human life. In *Humanae Vitae* ('Of Human Life') in 1968, Pope Paul VI reiterated traditional Catholic teaching. The sexual act, he wrote, must 'retain its intrinsic relationship to the procreation of human life'. So the use of condoms or the contraceptive pill remained unlawful for

Catholics because they directly contradicted the 'moral order which was established by God'. Furthermore, the Pope prohibited the 'direct interruption of the generative process already begun'. Abortion, even for therapeutic reasons, remained absolutely forbidden, as was sterilization.

By refusing to modify traditional teaching in this area – despite widespread pressure from lay Catholics and the pleadings of influential Catholic leaders – Pope Paul VI ensured that these particular distinctive teachings of Catholicism remained amongst its best known. In reality, many individual Catholics decided that, in good conscience, they could overlook the Pope's demands in these intensely personal areas. A survey completed in the 1990s of British Catholics concluded, for instance, that 'not a single voice was raised unambiguously in defence of *Humanae Vitae*' on the matter of artificial contraception, while 40 per cent of those questioned felt that in certain circumstances a woman could be justified morally in seeking an abortion.

However, successive popes have declined to retreat from Paul VI's restatement of traditional values. Some, like Pope John Paul II, have extended them into new areas of moral uncertainty – notably questions of *in vitro* fertilization and genetic manipulation, both of which Catholicism opposes and which we will explore at greater length in subsequent chapters. (*Roman Catholic Beliefs in England*, Michael Hornsby-Smith, Cambridge, 1991).

Conclusion

Catholicism, arguably alone of world religions, continues to suffer criticism for holding attitudes – especially in relation to sexual morality – that have long since been modified by secular society. One of the reasons for this is that so much of Catholic teaching is based on tradition – both in moral questions and in practices – which in its turn was dictated by the particular circumstances of particular eras. It is only by reading and studying the gospels, some Catholics argue, that a true picture of the correct behaviour for followers of Jesus in the modern world can be discerned.

part two

the history of Catholicism

03

the early Church

In this chapter you will learn:
- why Catholicism made its base in Rome
- how it grew into a Church
- how it became a political power.

There is, at first glance, an irony in the fact that Catholicism should be associated with Rome at all. Jesus lived and died in Palestine. How did a Middle Eastern religion end up with its global headquarters in Rome, especially since the Roman overlords of Jerusalem, in the shape of Pontius Pilate, were heavily involved in Jesus's execution?

The birth of the Catholic Church

In the immediate aftermath of the crucifixion, Jesus's original followers concentrated their preaching in Jerusalem among fellow Jews. However, a one-time persecutor of Jesus's disciples, Saul of Tarsus, underwent an extraordinary conversion experience on the road to Damascus where he saw a vision of Jesus. As a consequence, Saul became Paul and believed that Jesus's life, death and resurrection held a message that related not just to Jewish law and the prophecies of the Hebrew Scriptures (called the Old Testament by Christians), but to the whole human race. He therefore began to spread the word enthusiastically around the Roman Empire of which he (unlike the 12 original Apostles) was a citizen.

Paul was joined in this missionary endeavour by Peter, named by Jesus to lead his followers after his death. Antioch became the first centre of this outreach to the Gentiles – non-Jews – and it was here that the term Christian began to be used. 'It was at Antioch,' records the Acts of the Apostles (11.26) 'that the disciples were first called "Christians".'

In Jerusalem, such developments were regarded with concern by figures such as James, described in the New Testament as Jesus's brother (though according to Catholic tradition, in reality his step-brother, the son of Mary's husband, Joseph, who had been married before but whose first wife had died). James was the leader of Jesus's followers in the city, and believed that their future lay as a group within Judaism.

The tensions between these two approaches were only partially resolved by a compromise reached at a council, held in Jerusalem around AD 49. The momentum was strongly with Paul and Peter as they and their followers carried their wider interpretation of the teachings of Jesus to countless cities in the Roman Empire. This growth beyond Jewish roots became ever more marked with the destruction of the Temple in Jerusalem, spiritual home of Judaism, in AD 70 by the Roman occupiers.

The forces that were to make Christianity a world religion rather than a Jewish sect were gathering pace.

Rome, as capital of empire and a magnet for scholars, was the obvious place to base the new Church. However, it did not afford Jesus's followers a warm welcome. They preached against almost everything that the Roman Empire held dear – its morality, its religion, its celebration of war and its culture. The early Christians therefore quickly proved controversial, making converts but also suffering persecution and even death at the hands of those who regarded their teachings as wrong-headed and dangerous.

The early years of the Catholic Church were characterized by this constant, extraordinary growth which took place despite (and, some historians suggest, because of) violent opposition from the Roman authorities. Peter and Paul were just two amongst those martyred for their faith. One of the most remarkable features of the early centuries of the Church was its unshakeable faith in its own beliefs, something that enabled it to withstand such persecution. Tertullian (155–230), a noted Early Church leader, claimed that in the blood of martyrs was found the seed of the new Church.

Another noteworthy aspect was the foresight of leaders who, amid such outpourings of zeal and chaos, were able to lay the foundations of an enduring institution with shared beliefs and practices. It was a task that they undertook even though they were convinced that the Second Coming – the return in triumph of Jesus to earth – was imminent.

How the institution was created

There were three, often controversial, aspects to the work of the Early Church Fathers, as the first leaders of Christianity are known, in fashioning a Church:

1 The creation of a class of elders, who became by the second century deacons, priests and bishops, and who were eventually all-male.

2 The collecting of an authoritative set of apostolic writings, with the discarding of many other 'apocryphal' texts and gospels, a process that continued up to and including the fifth century Saint Jerome and his definitive Latin translation of the Bible, known as the *Vulgate*.

3 Reaching agreement on a set of basic beliefs by which Christians would live.

These three were not achieved quickly, without rancour, or even simultaneously. By AD 160, the system of hierarchical government that remains to this day a distinguishing feature of the Catholic Church had all but been established. One vital factor in this was the belief that each leader, 'ordained' to his ministry by the laying on of hands by those already 'ordained', could therefore trace a line back to Peter and hence Jesus. Again it is something that remains part of Catholic belief about its priesthood today.

The role of the Pope – and his supreme authority over the Church – had yet to be firmly established in practice (though it was endorsed in theory). It was only in the middle years of the fifth century, during the papacy of Leo the Great (one of only two popes to be accorded that title by Catholicism), that one can truly say the writ of the Bishop of Rome prevailed to any wide extent.

Agreement on a 'canon' of accepted writings also took several centuries. There were groups who took different views in the early centuries. The Gnostics, for example, derived from scripture an essentially pessimistic and 'dualistic' view of life on earth that saw the 'good' soul as trapped on earth in 'evil' human flesh. They therefore hankered after death and after-life. They were condemned as heretics and exiled from the new Church. Then there were those in the second century, for example, who felt that Saint John's Gospel, so different in tone and approach from the other three in the New Testament, should be excluded. Other 'gospels', ascribed amongst others to the Apostle Thomas – this basic account of his key sayings is thought to be the earliest written record of Jesus's life, produced within ten years of his death – were excluded, along with more impressionistic versions attributed to Judas Iscariot, Mary Magdalene and Philip. Consensus was not reached on such matters until towards the end of the fourth century.

The establishment of the rules by which Christians ought to live greatly preoccupied Early Church Fathers such as Irenaeus of Lyons (130–202) in his widely circulated writings, as well as the regular 'synods' or meetings of bishops from all the centres of Christianity. It was the Council of Nicaea (325) which finally agreed a creed or statement of key beliefs, known ever after as the *Nicene Creed*.

The word 'catholic', meaning universal, was used very early on in Christianity's history to denote its ambitions to be the religion of all. A letter written by Saint Ignatius of Antioch (d.107) to Christians in the Greek city of Smyrna just before his death, for example, contains the term 'Catholic Church'. By it, Ignatius was describing Christianity in its universal sense, but excluding heretics, such as those who reject the idea that 'the Eucharist [is] the flesh of our Saviour Jesus Christ, which suffered for our sins'. It is seen in other second-century texts such as *The Martyrdom of Polycarp*, an account of the burning to death in 155 of a revered Christian leader by Romans in front of a crowd because he refused to renounce his religion, and again in the 'Muratorian Fragment', believed to be the earliest surviving list of the books of the New Testament, dating back to 177.

Catholicism as a state religion

As the far-flung Roman Empire came under sustained attack from Barbarian forces in the fourth century, successive imperial leaders tried to scapegoat Christians as the root of the trouble. Emperor Diocletian in 303, for example, ordered all Christian places of worship to be laid to waste and their holy books burnt. But it was a losing fight for the soul of the empire and in 312 Constantine attributed his latest victory in battle to the Christian God. The age of persecution was over. His subsequent generosity towards the Catholic Church saw state patronage make possible the first appearance of mighty basilicas in Rome, including that at Saint John Lateran, the mother church of the city, and until 1308 home to the popes.

It was as 'Catholic Christians' that Jesus's followers entered Roman imperial law when Theodosius I (379–95) designated the name for adherents of 'that religion which was delivered to the Romans by the divine Apostle Peter, as it has been preserved by faithful tradition and which is now professed by the Pontiff [Pope] Damasus'. This law, dated 380, established Catholic Christianity as the official religion of the Roman Empire.

With acceptance as part of the state came the opportunity for Catholicism to play a greater and more open role in the community. There were visible places of worship, with a standardized liturgy – an early and immediately recognizable form of the Mass, a term used from the fifth century onwards. A liturgical calendar of feast days was established, with particular emphasis placed on Christmas, marking the birth of Jesus, and especially on Easter when his death and resurrection were commemorated. And the seven sacraments began to be consolidated, in a process not wholly completed until the early Middle Ages.

By the end of the fourth century, Christianity was the religion of the majority of Roman citizens, but the Empire itself was collapsing. As it did, the Church stepped into the vacuum, assuming temporal as well as spiritual authority. Bishops, for example, took charge of the care of the poor in their cities, and came to be seen as the most powerful individuals within their walls, building a new social order out of the wreckage of the Empire.

The growth of papal power

Pope Leo the Great (440–61) is best remembered for his insistence on the supreme authority of the papacy in the Church, moving Catholicism from a system of largely autonomous prelates and bishops, widely scattered about the lands of the old Empire, to the hierarchical model of governance known today. But under Leo, Christianity also grew in influence and importance in the secular sphere. In 452, as Pope, he confronted Attila the Hun (then laying waste to northern Italy and preparing to head south towards Rome) and persuaded him to withdraw.

Such a success did not endure and Rome faced wave after wave of invaders. The Emperor was now based in Constantinople in the East, with only an Exarch at Ravenna, on the eastern Adriatic coast of Italy, representing imperial power in the West. In Rome, the popes assumed command of the city and surrounding lands, a situation that was to endure for almost 1400 years.

Among the civil administrators of the city from 572 to 574 was Gregory, who came of a local noble family that had already provided two popes. Gregory (c.540–604) abandoned all worldly goods on the death of his father and adopted the new monastic style of life. This had been growing in influence all across the Catholic Church in imitation of the 'Desert Fathers', hermits and ascetics such as Saint Antony (c.251–356) who from the third century onwards dedicated their lives to prayer and hard manual labour in loosely-knit communities in the Egyptian desert.

Their example inspired others, like Benedict of Nursia (480–547), whose 'Rule' lead to the foundation of monasteries in Italy and eventually throughout Europe. These institutions housed men following regimented, celibate lives of prayer, service and learning, and earned widespread public respect. Fiercely loyal to the papacy, the new generation of monks were key figures in extending the Pope's authority.

Gregory was summoned out of his monastery in 590 and elected, by popular acclaim of Roman citizens, as the new Pope. The first monk-pope, he is the second of the popes known by the title 'the Great'. His lasting achievements in the history of Catholicism were fourfold:

1 He firmly established the papacy as the key political power in Rome and central Italy.
2 He insisted that his word, as Pope, took precedence throughout the Western Christian Church (there were still Patriarchs – or leaders – with much independence in Antioch, Constantinople, Alexandria and Jerusalem). 'I know of no bishop who is not subject to the Apostolic See when fault has been committed,' Gregory wrote.
3 He was vigorous in sending out his fellow monks as missionaries to modern-day Germany, France and Scandinavia to convert pagans to Catholicism. His envoys included Augustine of Canterbury who, in 597, arrived in England and converted King Ethelbert of Kent.
4 In his many writings on theology and spirituality, such as his *Dialogues*, he summarized the basis for Christian thought in a way that remained popular up to the mediaeval period.

To the foundations of power, authority and belief that Gregory and his successors had laid, Pope Stephen II (752–7), another scion of a Roman aristocratic family, added a final vital element. In 753 he crossed the Alps to forge an alliance with the Frankish King Pepin. In return for the papal blessing, Pepin granted the papacy political control of much of central Italy, and guaranteed it with his own army. When Pepin's son, Charlemagne, managed to establish his own rule over the European lands that had once constituted the western part of the Roman Empire, he came to Rome in 800 and knelt before Pope Leo III (795–816) to be 'crowned by God' as Holy Roman Emperor. The alliance of the Catholic Church with earthly rulers that was to dominate Europe was now firmly established.

Key thinkers in the first millennium of Catholicism

Along with Pope Gregory the Great, Catholicism hails three other figures among the Fathers of the Church in its first millennium as 'doctors' or great teachers.

1 **Saint Ambrose** (334–97) A Roman governor who was elected Bishop of Milan in 374 by popular acclaim, Ambrose faced down heresy within the Church and forced the Emperor, Theodosius I, to do public penance for ordering a massacre of rioters, insisting that 'the Emperor is within the Church: he is not above it'. His principal legacy, though, was his collected sermons; practical guidelines to believers on the sacraments of baptism, Eucharist and confirmation. A keen advocate of church music, he is credited with introducing it into liturgy.

2 **Saint Augustine of Hippo** (354–430) Baptized a Christian, Augustine drifted away from the Church as a young man and led a worldly and debauched life. However, in 387 he was inspired to return by Ambrose, among others, and served for the rest of his years as an outstanding and admired bishop and teacher in North Africa. His writings – particularly his *Confessions* and *City of God* – have ensured him a central place in Catholicism thereafter, and are still regularly quoted by popes and bishops. Drawing on his own past, Augustine dwelt at length on the sinfulness of human flesh and the dangers for the spirit of human sexuality. His legacy can be seen in Catholicism's distinctive teachings on sex and, some of his critics argue, in its negative attitudes to women.

3 **Saint Jerome** (342–420) A one-time hermit who travelled extensively, spending time in Antioch, Bethlehem and Constantinople, he was secretary to Pope Damasus I (366–84) who commissioned him to translate from Greek into Latin the gospel texts, a task which grew into compiling the whole of the Bible in Latin in his *Vulgate* (i.e. the vulgar tongue, the scriptures made accessible in the language of the people) completed only in 404. The pre-eminent biblical scholar in Catholicism, often represented by the figure of a lion, his letters and polemical writings also contributed to emerging ideas on doctrine.

04

from the Dark Ages to the Reformation

In this chapter you will learn:

- how the popes came to dominate Europe
- about the role of the Inquisition
- about the abuses that precipitated the Reformation.

The history of the Catholic Church, and in particular the history of the papacy, is a tale of peaks and troughs of power and influence in an ever-shifting and often all-absorbing relationship with secular authorities. The link between Church and state, symbolized by Leo placing the imperial crown on Charlemagne's head in the name of God, became a key factor in both world history, and in the story of Catholicism.

The rise to European domination

That crowning of Charlemagne by Pope Leo III marked a high point for the alliance of Church and state that was at the heart of the new Holy Roman Empire. Charlemagne's heirs, however, lacked his gifts as a politician and warrior and ended up fighting amongst themselves. The Empire collapsed.

The papacy, too, went into decline in the ninth century, a period known to history as the Dark Ages. The successors to Saint Peter abandoned their ambition to rule a Europe-wide Church and concentrated instead only on Rome. They were chosen by and from local Roman families who wanted popes capable of governing their unruly and corrupt city.

Two particular low points in this period were the legendary election of a German woman of English descent called Joan, disguised as a man, to the papal throne in 853, and the subjugation of the office of Pope to the ambitions of a ruthless and immoral Roman matriarch, Marozia, who installed a succession of her lovers and offspring on St Peter's throne during the tenth century in an era later characterized as a 'pornocracy'.

The legend of Pope Joan

The She-Pope's story is recorded by some 500 chroniclers of the papacy, from the twelfth century until the end of the seventeenth century. The authors include several papal servants and bishops, but none is an eyewitness or even near contemporary of Pope John VIII (853–5). One of the most distinguished, Martin of Poland, writing in 1277, states that John was excluded from 'the catalogue of holy popes, as well on account of her female sex as on account of the foul nature of the transaction'. John was in fact, Martin of Poland recounts, a learned German woman and the child of English missionaries, who had first disguised herself as a monk to continue her education, but who had been so successful that she had attracted the patronage of her predecessor, Pope Leo IV, and was elected his successor by popular acclaim. Her gender was, however, discovered only when she fell pregnant and gave birth in the street when travelling from the Lateran Palace, then the home of popes, to the Vatican. The accounts variously describe her as being stoned to death, along with her baby, or tied to the legs of a horse and dragged through the street until dead. The legend was an accepted if never celebrated part of Catholic tradition until the Reformation when, faced by dissidents using it to damn all claims of papal authority, the Catholic Church dismissed Pope Joan as the invention of Protestant forgers. The story has, however, lived on, in fiction, in art and in feminist readings of history.

In conflict with ambitious princes

One of Marozia's descendants, the dissolute John XII (Pope 955–64), elected at the age of just 18, was Pope at the time when Charlemagne's empire underwent a revival under the Saxon leader, Otto the Great (912–73). Otto first forced John to crown him Holy Roman Emperor in 962 and then demonstrated his dominance over a weakened papacy by deposing him. This remained a pattern in Catholicism for the next 100 years. Any pope who showed any independence – such as Benedict IX (1032–48) – risked being supplanted by imperial whim with nominees who are now usually described by Catholicism as 'anti-popes'.

The papacy lost any effective control over who became bishops. 'Lay investiture' – selection of local Church leaders by the Emperor or princes – became a symbol of the papacy's subjugation. Alongside political weakness went moral decline. There was a thriving trade in spiritual goods – up to and including appointment as a bishop or papal servant – that is known as simony, as well as a general lack of discipline among the clergy in both public and private matters. Priests would marry and then discard wives, while their children would lay claim to Church lands. Even the revered monastic movement fell into disrepute.

From the mid-eleventh century onwards, however, Catholicism started to put its house in order. There was a growing move towards enforcing celibacy on all priests – as a way, in part, of avoiding their descendants claiming Church lands. Monastic reforms were epitomized by Bernard of Clairvaux (1090–1153) who advocated a more primitive form of monastic observance. And the papacy began to reassert its independence and win back its place as the equal of temporal rulers, even coming to dominate them. A Church decree of 1059 officially excluded both the Emperor and Roman nobles from any role in electing a new pope, but it fell to Pope Gregory VII (1073–85) to enforce it. He laid out his cherished notion of papal monarchy in *Dictatus Papae* of 1075. 'The Pope can be judged by no one; the Roman Church has never erred and will never err till the end of time; the Roman Church was founded by Christ alone; the Pope alone can depose and restore bishops; he alone can make new laws.'

He gave such ambitions practical expression by standing up to the Emperor, Henry IV, over appointments, excommunicating him (throwing him out of the Church) when he refused to accept the Pope's wishes, and then embarking on a long war with Henry that left Rome in ruins. The battle had not been won by the time of Gregory's death. Indeed, he was in exile from Rome, but under Urban II (1088–99) victory was completed.

Schism with the East

Alongside curbing the influence of outsiders in the running of the Catholic Church, the papacy in this period also reasserted its supreme authority internally. Leo IX (1048–54) was a key figure in this restoration, using tours, councils and writings to impose his beliefs on his Church and bishops, and to clamp down on corruption. The loyalty of the reinvigorated monastic orders to the papacy considerably strengthened its hand over any local prelates with independent ideas, while the wiping out of the Christian Church in North Africa – traditionally resistant to Roman dictate – by the rapid spread of Islam along the southern coast of the Mediterranean had the by-product of removing another obstacle to papal ambitions. The ancient patriarchates of Antioch, Alexandria and Jerusalem all fell into decline.

The Pope in Rome now had only one internal rival for domination of the universal Catholic Church, the Patriarch of Constantinople. The relationship between Western and Eastern parts of Christianity had long been a delicate one. There was a number of schisms, but each was eventually patched up. In the eighth century, for example, there was a dispute between the two over Iconoclasm – Constantinople's desire to abolish the use of religious images. Rome objected. Eventually a compromise was found. Each dispute, however, weakened the ties that bound the Eastern Church to the papacy until in practice it seemed content to pay nominal homage to Rome while in theory acting as a self-sufficient and autonomous body.

That tolerance came to an end in the time of Patriarch Michael Cerularius (1043–58). He was impatient with the paramount authority of the papacy, especially when exercised in certain questions concerning the liturgy, and responded by withdrawing permission for the Latin rite of the Western Church to be celebrated in areas under his authority. Pope Leo IX (Pope 1049–54) answered by banning the Greek rite of the Eastern Church in parts of southern Italy ruled by the Byzantine Emperor, based in Constantinople.

The dispute escalated with intemperate papal envoys in Constantinople trying to excommunicate Michael Cerularius. Trust between the Pope and the Patriarch reached a low ebb and remained there when, in 1095, Pope Urban called for a crusade to relieve the pressure Islam was placing on beleaguered Christians in the eastern Mediterranean. When Antioch was retaken in 1098, the Crusaders evicted the Greek Patriarch, loyal to Constantinople, and replaced him with a Latin one, owing his allegiance only to the Pope.

The breach between the two parts of the Catholic family deepened. Matters reached a head during the Fourth Crusade (1202–4), when the Western knights became embroiled in the power struggle of a pretender to the Eastern Emperor's throne. They entered Constantinople and sacked churches there. As a result, Christianity fractured. Attempts were made in 1274 and 1439 to heal the wound, but henceforth the Catholic West and the Orthodox East went their own ways.

Innocent III – The Vicar of Christ

Arguably the most ambitious of the papal monarchs was Innocent III (1198–1216). He was the first Pope to describe himself as 'the Vicar of Christ', someone, as he put it, who 'sat midway between God and man, below God but above man'. This person – the Pope – had, in Innocent's words, 'not only the universal Church but the whole world to govern'. It is a claim still made by today's pontiffs who use the title 'Vicar of Jesus Christ'.

Innocent, however, wanted more than titles. He wished to build a system of morality, centred on himself, that would regulate the whole gamut of human behaviour across the known world. This ambition prompted a huge growth in the range and use of Canon – or Church – Law in an effort to define precisely how each and every Catholic ought to live their lives. In 1215 Innocent summoned the Fourth Council of the Lateran which established such enduring Catholic practices as the obligation to attend the sacraments of Confession and Eucharist at least once a year, and set out entry qualifications for candidates for the clergy in an attempt to address the abuses of some rogue priests.

It was no good, Innocent realized, telling people what to do if you could not make them obey, so he also strengthened the curia – or Rome-based Church bureaucracy – so that it could enforce his writ. He also promoted the system, still in existence in Catholicism today, by which all bishops had to make regular (usually five-yearly) *ad limina* visits to Rome to meet the Pope. The phrase *ad limina* translates as 'to the threshold' and refers to visiting the 'threshold of the Apostles', or the burial place of Saint Peter in Rome. The claim of Apostolic Succession remained at the root of the papacy's authority, notwithstanding the behaviour of some of the popes themselves. It is, however, for commissioning the Inquisition that Innocent is best remembered.

The Inquisition

The Inquisition was established in 1208 as a key instrument of papal government. It consisted of special tribunals charged with rooting out heresy across Europe. Initially it focused on southern France where the Cathars (or Albigensians), who took their name from the Greek for 'unpolluted', were a group of Catholics living simple, celibate lives. They refused to fall in line with the papacy, regarding Rome as bloated and corrupt. When pressed by Innocent's representative to change their minds, they responded by killing the papal legate.

This killing resulted in the establishment of the Inquisition. Innocent had tired of persuasion and was resorting to coercion. There was nothing in the New Testament to support the methods the Inquisition employed, but he drew on the Old Testament, as well as writers such as Saint Augustine, to justify his innovation. Cathars were tortured – often having their eyes gouged out – in an effort to make them see the sinfulness of their lives. Those who refused (and many who acceded) were killed as 'Devil-worshippers'.

Such was its success in stamping out this particular 'heresy' that, in 1233, the Inquisition was given a permanent place in the Catholic Church. Neither local bishops nor local courts had any power to resist it. Victims were accused on the basis of anonymous denunciations, and seldom had the chance to organize a defence before they were subjected to torture. The activities of the Inquisitors, many of them initially Dominican friars, demonstrated the Church's claim to a jurisdiction that overruled both state and individual conscience. As its ambitions grew, the Church allowed the Inquisition to target any group that was perceived as standing in the way of complete Catholic hegemony in Europe – be they pagans, Jews or even women. All suffered similar demonization by the Inquisition, creating a reign of terror during which many abuses occurred.

The Spanish Inquisition came later, starting in 1478 and only being swept away in 1808 when Napoleon invaded Spain. It alone claimed over 100,000 victims. It differed from the mediaeval Inquisition in that it was run by the Spanish crown, with the papacy on several occasions intervening to urge clemency (and being ignored). In one particularly gruesome form of torture, prisoners' hands would be tied behind their backs and their bodies then hoisted off the ground. They would be left suspended for hours or days until they were ready to 'confess' their sins. In another, the accused would be strapped to a trestle table, with their feet higher than their heads, while the priestly inquisitors would pour water down their throats.

Avignon popes

Innocent's reign marked the high point of papal power in the wider European context. The prince he had hand-picked to become the next Holy Roman Emperor, Frederick II of Sicily (1194–1250), was anything but compliant with papal demands and engaged in a long and bitter battle for supremacy with first Gregory IX (1227–41) and then the candidate he had himself chosen as Gregory's successor but one, Innocent IV (1243–54).

However, the greatest threat to papal authority over the Church increasingly came not from Germany but from France, where Philip IV 'the Fair' (1268–1314) clashed repeatedly with Pope Boniface VIII (1294–1303), even trying to kidnap the pontiff and bring him to France where he would be forced to abdicate. Boniface avoided this fate, but his successor but one, Clement V

(1305–14), did not share his resilience and bowed to Philip's demand to relocate himself, and the papacy, in Avignon in southern France. He was the first of seven 'Avignon popes', leading the Church between 1305 and 1378 but, in practice, subjugating it to the French monarchy.

When the papacy finally managed to return to Rome, urged on by figures such as Catherine of Siena (1347–80), and reassert its independence, it was immediately plunged into the Forty Year Schism with the election of the unstable and tyrannical Urban VI in 1378. By now there was a group of senior churchmen, known as cardinals, who were able to exert influence from within the Church on the Pope. The first cardinals had existed in ninth-century Rome, as the heads of the city's most important churches, but by the twelfth century they had spread throughout the Catholic world. Among their powers was that of election of the Pope.

After Urban had demonstrated his autocratic tendencies, the cardinals were split between those who felt they had no choice but to follow the man they had elected, and those who appealed to the French monarch for support in deposing him in favour of Clement VII, a candidate more to their taste. Both groups refused to back down, so there were two popes – one in Rome and one in Avignon. In 1409, the cardinals held a council at Pisa and agreed to depose both ruling popes, and replace them with an alternative, Alexander V. But the two incumbents refused to go and, as Alexander was now in office, Catholicism had three popes.

The matter was finally solved at the Council of Constance in 1414. All three popes were removed in favour of Martin V, a candidate acceptable to all parties. Part of the compromise was the imposition of a more collective style of leadership on the Church, with popes directed to consult with their cardinals on the crucial questions of reform that were facing Catholicism.

Corruption, simony, high ecclesiastical taxes and the debacle of having three popes simultaneously had all sapped the Church's authority. Yet, rather than attack the root causes, popes and cardinals preferred to indulge in a running battle for authority that was never quite resolved. It left the Church weakened as it faced new threats after the Ottoman Turks had taken Constantinople in 1453 and began advancing into Europe.

Thomas Aquinas

Saint Thomas Aquinas (1225–74) is regarded by many as the greatest of all Catholic theologians. Educated by the Benedictines in Italy, he became a Dominican friar. Aquinas was convinced that faith and reason were compatible. 'For the knowledge of any truth whatsoever,' he wrote, 'man needs divine help, that the intellect may be moved by God to its act.' To prove the point, he returned to the philosophers of Ancient Greece, notably Aristotle (384–322 BC), and borrowed from their ideas to create a rational understanding of God as the creator and source of all being, goodness and truth, who is present in us all.

Aquinas left as his most significant gift to the Church the *Summa Theologia* (1266–74), a systematic exposition of theology, based on reason, which earned him the title 'universal teacher'. He described four kinds of law: eternal, natural, human and divine. Eternal law is the decree of God that governs all creation. Natural law is the human 'participation' in the eternal law and is discovered by reason. Natural law ensures that 'good is to be done and promoted, and evil is to be avoided'. This belief in a preordained, moral pattern of behaviour, learnt by observing (as he had) the behaviour of animals, continues to guide Catholic attitudes. Still influential is his defence of priestly celibacy – 'the state of virginity is preferable to that of even continent marriage'.

Impression of power

In the late fifteenth century, the Renaissance papacy gave every outward impression of being more powerful than ever. The show of wealth, the commissioning of great works of art that are part of the Catholic treasury to this day, and the flamboyant lifestyles of some popes suggested an institution in rude health. The reality, however, was that Catholicism was in moral and spiritual decline. Political power and personal gain mattered more to Church leaders than principles. Alexander VI (1492–1503), sometimes called the 'Borgia Pope', was, for example, installed as Pope with his various children looking on.

Despairing of Rome and the papacy, there were many local reform movements that aimed at restoring the public esteem of the clergy, recapturing the high ideals of the monasteries, and even empowering the laity – such as the brotherhood founded in 1497 in Genoa by Ettore Vernazza and known as the Oratory of

Divine Love. It sought spiritual renewal by dedication to prayer, meditation and acts of charity, and spread to Rome, Naples and Bologna.

None, however, was sufficient to turn back the outbreak of dissatisfaction that was to divide Christianity. When an Augustinian monk and teacher, Martin Luther (1483–1546), questioned the corruption and the simony, his attack precipitated a wider crisis. There was a theological basis to Luther's rebellion. He rejected the notion, central to Catholicism then and now, that by doing good works you could earn salvation after death. Such an idea, Luther felt, was simply an invitation to ego. Salvation came through faith in God. It was not an individual's holiness than counted. It was God's love.

Luther's criticism broadened to take in other aspects of Catholicism. He emphasized the importance of a personal relationship with God, rather than one conducted through the intermediary of a priest, and he constantly referred to the Bible rather than to the traditional practices and interpretations of the Church. However, his position was not so very far from Catholicism on many subjects that he inevitably had to cause a schism. It was the context in which he launched his onslaught that led to that.

His programme – according to legend set out in the 95 theses he nailed to the door of the castle church in Wittenberg in October 1517, but more likely to have been contained in a letter he sent to his bishop, and then circulated when he received no reply – certainly had a popular appeal. His attack in particular on the sale of indulgences – the idea that if you paid the Church money, it could mitigate your sins, or those of friends and relatives already dead and awaiting God's final judgement – struck a chord with all those who felt the Church had grown corrupt in linking financial and spiritual matters. Indulgences were sold, for example, to fund the building of a new Saint Peter's Basilica, finally started in 1608.

The theses of Martin Luther

Four of the 95 theses

1 The true treasure of the Church is the Most Holy Gospel of the glory and the grace of God.

2 To think the papal pardons so great that they could absolve a man even if he had committed an impossible sin and violated the Mother of God – this is madness.

3 To say that the cross, emblazoned with the papal arms, is of equal worth with the Cross of Christ is blasphemy.

4 Why does not the Pope, whose wealth is today greater than the riches of the richest, build just one church of Saint Peter with his own money, rather than with the money of poor believers?

Luther was also an adept orator who used advances in printing techniques to get his message to a wide audience. He was treated far too casually at first by an arrogant papacy and its bishops. They began by dismissing his protests, unable to see that he was speaking for a large constituency. Then when Rome felt Luther needed to be answered, it produced a response, in 1520, widely condemned as vague, weak and full of personal invective.

Rome also failed to see that Luther's revolt could be exploited by princes who – however sincerely they may have agreed or disagreed with what he was saying – saw an opportunity to curtail the power and claims of the papacy over their domains. The protection offered by Frederick, the Elector of Saxony, ensured that Luther didn't end up silenced or killed by the Inquisition.

As Luther's popularity grew, he was emboldened to extend his attack into a full-scale assault on the papacy and the whole concept of the Apostolic Succession. He also rejected five of the seven sacraments, limiting himself to Baptism and Eucharist (albeit with the notion of transubstantiation tempered), and advocated a pared-down liturgy delivered not in Latin but in the local language so as to make it accessible.

Summoned by Charles V, the Holy Roman Emperor (1500–58), before the Diet (assembly) of Worms in 1521, Luther refused to recant because my 'conscience is held captive to the Word of God'. The Emperor, who had vowed to stamp out heresy, was prevented by the German princes from acting decisively against Luther. Again their motives were both spiritual and political. The new Lutheranism was taken up in some German cities. Catholic Christendom was once more divided.

At first it was believed to be a temporary division, but the structures of Lutheranism grew quickly, especially in the absence of the Emperor who was heavily involved in affairs in Spain from 1521 to 1530. The best chance at reconciliation came in 1541 at Regensburg, based on conceding to the Lutherans (also known as Protestants) a married clergy and freedom from papal jurisdiction while still recognizing papal primacy, but Rome could not agree to give so much ground.

Luther's ideas therefore spread across Europe and inspired a variety of reformed or Protestant churches to spring up. In England, Henry VIII (1491–1547), hitherto a staunch supporter of the papacy, embraced the new Protestant spirit to resolve a dispute over divorcing his first wife and marrying Anne Boleyn, as part of his determination to have a male heir. Subsequent English monarchs swung between extreme Protestantism – Edward VI (1537–53) – and aggressive Catholicism – Mary I (1516–58) – until Henry's daughter, Elizabeth (1533–1603) built a consensus around a moderate form of Protestantism in the Church of England, retaining such aspects of Catholicism as bishops.

Conclusion

The high water mark of Catholic influence in Europe had been reached. Its political ambitions had weakened the papacy's moral authority, and its intolerance of dissent had cost it dearly. The Reformation finally destroyed the outward show of unity that bound together Catholic Europe. It was as much a political as a theological revolution. Henceforth, the Catholic Church would be one among several branches of the Christian family.

05

Counter-Reformation to Holocaust

In this chapter you will learn:

- how Catholicism recovered from the Reformation
- how it was attacked by Enlightenment thinkers
- how it retreated from the modern world.

In the years after Luther's revolt, over half of Europe's believers, according to some documents, turned their back on Rome. It was the greatest crisis ever to face the Catholic Church and its leaders. The result could simply have been that Catholicism withered on the vine. Instead it came back renewed and refocused, with a cautious, traditional and often deeply suspicious view of the world in which it operated.

The Counter-Reformation

Not everything that happened in the Catholic Church after the Reformation can be put down to a reaction against Luther. There were already areas of new growth that pre-dated 1517, often small groups, or brotherhoods, dedicated to cleansing the priesthood and encouraging the better administration of the Church. It is in such groups that we find the origins of the Jesuits, started by the Spaniard, Ignatius Loyola (1491–1556), in Paris in 1534 and granted papal approval in 1540. There, too, can be seen the roots of the Capuchins, an offshoot of the Franciscans, aiming to return the order to its original goals, and founded in 1528. They were soon a familiar sight with their coarse robes and large square hoods. These two groups – Jesuits and Capuchins – were among the leaders of the Counter-Reformation.

The fight-back began in December 1545 with the opening of a council in the northern Italian city of Trent. The actual meetings took no more than three years, but were spread out over 18 years while the new programme was agreed. Consensus was finally reached in 1563 and the Council of Trent addressed head-on some of Luther's most damaging accusations:

1 It restated the Catholic belief that both scripture *and* tradition play their parts in shaping faith and a moral life.
2 It rejected the notion of justification by faith alone, and insisted on the need for hope and charity, especially in the form of good works.
3 It maintained that the seven sacraments – not just two – all had divine validity.
4 It insisted that henceforth all those wanting to be priests should be celibate, and should be trained according to strict and strictly enforced central rules in seminaries, run by local bishops.

5 It endorsed the hierarchical model of the Church, with the Pope wielding supreme authority and local bishops controlling their diocese, priests and laity.

6 It reformed the Mass, leading to the issuing in 1570 of the *Missale Romanum* – the Roman Missal which held sway until the 1960s – with a rigid liturgical formula, to be followed everywhere and known as the Tridentine rite.

There had, of course, been reforming councils in the past. The test of Trent was not its ambitions, but how effectively they were implemented. The post-Reformation papacy was blessed in this regard by figures like Pius V (1566–72), a morally upright, monkish former Inquisitor, who rooted out corruption in the Curia and led by personal example. He promoted his *Catechism* as a basic guide to the good Catholic life, revived the Inquisition (which had been in decline outside Spain) as a way of maintaining discipline, and in 1571 produced an *Index of Condemned Books* to guide Catholic readers away from texts likely to corrupt them.

The successes of the Counter-Reformation were not simply down to one man, however. A generation of energetic bishops in their dioceses spearheaded the strengthening of Catholicism at local level, ably assisted by the Capuchins, Jesuits and other religious orders. Loyola's *Spiritual Exercises* – a vigorous combination of inner prayer and spirituality with external hard work and determination – inspired not just his followers but many others throughout the Church and continues to do so to this day. Taking seriously Trent's commitment to good works playing their part in faith, the Jesuits and other religious orders took up the challenge with gusto to care for the poor, to run schools, to encourage learning through universities, and to export the faith as missionaries to the 'New World' that had opened up following the American discoveries of Christopher Columbus after 1492. It was a Jesuit, Francis Xavier (1506–52) who carried Catholicism first to Portuguese India at Goa in 1542 and then to Japan and China.

The net effect of this Counter-Reformation revival was to see Catholicism restored to lands where it had been displaced by the new Protestantism. In Poland, France, the southern Netherlands and parts of Germany, it regained its former influence.

Jansenism and Gallicanism

By the middle of the seventeenth century, the immediate post-Reformation map had been redrawn. Catholicism had expanded once again at the expense of Protestantism, but the two sides had reached a stalemate. Henceforth the greatest threats to the Catholic Church came from within, in the form of internal dissidents, and from outside, with the rise of an intellectual movement in the Enlightenment which had little time for traditional religion.

The Catholic Bishop, Cornelius Jansen of Ypres (1585–1638), preached and wrote at length on the essential corruption of human nature. His pessimistic view of human sinfulness, rooted in the notion of the inheritance of Original Sin from Adam and Eve, owed much, Jansen admitted, to Saint Augustine of Hippo. The Jesuits, however, saw in Jansen's writings the influence of Protestant thought about humanity being totally subject to God's will. They condemned him and his followers – the Jansenists – with the backing of the papacy and the French Crown.

The involvement of the Pope and the French monarch gave the dispute a wider resonance, with those who disputed papal claims of jurisdiction and political opponents of the king rallying to the Jansenist cause. An essentially theological dispute took on a political dimension. Official condemnation came from Rome, but the clash continued to create divisions, especially in France and the Low Countries.

Also of French origin was Gallicanism, which sought a return to the pre-Reformation pattern of cardinals and Pope *jointly* running the Church, and therefore rejected Roman centralization and over-arching papal claims. A German version of the same movement was known as Febronianism.

Again it provided an opportunity for those with axes to grind to get involved. Louis XIV (1638–1715) gave support to Gallicanism, bringing him into a prolonged and bitter struggle with Pope Innocent XI (1676–1689). With the French Bourbons vying with the Hapsburgs in Spain and Germany for influence on the political stage of Europe, the papacy in this period often found itself the subject of intrigue between the two ruling families, with each trying to ensure its candidate was elected to Saint Peter's throne. Such machinations served only to weaken the Pope's authority.

That muddled and muddied world of competing secular influences, exploiting internal divisions within Catholicism, played a significant part in the closing down of the Jesuits in 1773. The Society of Jesus – to give Loyola's followers their correct name – had made many enemies in their role as front-line crusaders of the Counter-Reformation, arch defenders of papal influence. When, in the eighteenth century, the Society became involved in financial and political scandals in France and in controversy on account of its social experiments in the New World that angered the Spanish monarchs, their opponents pressed the papacy to take action.

In France, the Jesuits were abolished by royal decree in 1764. They were expelled from Spain in 1767. Pope Clement XIII (1758–1769) resisted these moves fiercely but, in the election that followed his death, Bourbon and Hapsburg pressure ensured a pope, Clement XIV (1769–74), who soon saw he had no choice but to bow to royal wishes. In 1773 the Jesuits were disbanded.

The Enlightenment

The fall of the Jesuits was greeted as a great triumph for Enlightenment thinking. Hitherto, in the history of Catholicism, the most formidable intellectual challenges had come from thinkers within its ranks, some of whom, like Luther, had then left. The growth in Enlightenment thinking from the mid-seventeenth and through the eighteenth century confronted the Church with enemies from without who rejected everything it stood for. Humankind need no longer, the Enlightenment thinkers wrote, feel at odds with their world, under threat and therefore in need of the Church's protection. Events that had, in the past, been attributed to God's intervention in the world were now being explained rationally by a new generation of scientists.

The Enlightenment challenged Catholicism on its home ground – questions of human nature, our place in the universe, history and morality. Europe was experiencing the dawn of secular culture, with its roots not in the Bible or Church tradition, but rather in science and human experience. Catholicism's instinctive and defensive reaction was to condemn. When devout thinkers such as Galileo Galilei (1564–1642) tried to ease the Church into a new world where the earth was no longer the centre of everything, but a sphere travelling around the sun, they were rejected. Galileo was condemned as a heretic in 1633.

The new ideas of rationalism, religious freedom and personal autonomy that came with the Enlightenment threatened Catholicism in the same way that its own teachings had once threatened the bedrock of the Roman Empire. They were the antithesis of everything Catholicism held dear. In particular, the Church disliked the optimism about human nature and progress that was part of the Enlightenment. So they lashed out. Voltaire's *Dictionnaire Philosophique* of 1764, for example, was ordered to be burned in both France and Rome.

The French Revolution

The French Revolution was, in one sense, the product of Enlightenment thinking. Efforts to reform the government of France to increase popular participation started with a gathering of representatives at Versailles in the spring of 1789. The French Catholic Church and the papacy were not wholly opposed to such change. Some clergy took part in the assembly and voted for the proposed reforms, but as events gathered momentum and swept away the monarchy and the whole social order, organized religion itself inevitably came under attack. Church lands were confiscated and clergy were required to take an oath of allegiance to the new French republic.

This raised the age-old issue of the Church's relationship with the state. Pope Pius VI (1775–99), ordered the clergy to refuse the oath. He gave his blessing to the coalition of countries gathering to bring down the Revolution and was punished for it when the triumphant French forces under Napoleon Bonaparte invaded the Papal States in 1796.

In February 1798 the French seized Rome and deposed Pius as head of state. He died in exile the following year, but the cardinals, meeting in Venice, under Austrian protection, elected Pius VII (1800–23), a more moderate figure, who declared there was no inevitable conflict between Catholicism and democracy. He returned to Rome and in 1801 agreed a Concordat with the French, headed by the now First Counsel Bonaparte, which recognized Catholicism as the religion of the majority of the French. Three years later the Pope travelled to Paris to crown Bonaparte as Emperor, but their accommodation was short-lived. When Napoleon took on the rest of Europe, Pius declared himself neutral. The outraged Emperor retook Rome in 1809 and thereafter held the Pope captive until his defeat in 1815.

Retreat from a changing world

In the peace that followed, Pius emerged with honour for having enraged Bonaparte. As a result he was able to roll back state incursions on his authority and so reclaim the right to name bishops. Moreover, he was recognized once again as ruler of the Papal States. He even managed to re-establish the Jesuits with little opposition from governments.

There was a new energy and confidence in Catholicism, but as the century progressed it increasingly grew alarmed by the pace of change in the world, and sided with an Old Order that was in decline in the face of liberal, democratic, economic and secular pressures. In the 1820s, though, there were great hopes that a more liberal form of Catholicism would grow in harmony with the new liberal mood in Europe, especially amongst the professional middle classes. The leading advocates of such a development were figures like the Breton priest, Felicite de Lamennais (1782–1854), who argued for the separation of Church and state as a way of freeing Catholicism from the baggage and concerns of the past, and thereby offering the chance to engage more closely with the lives of those in the pews.

De Lamennais supported religious freedom, freedom of the press and universal suffrage, arguing that the Church had nothing to fear and much to gain from such liberal demands. He attracted much popular support but in 1832 was roundly denounced by Pope Gregory XVI (1831–46) in his encyclical *Mirari Vos* – 'On Liberalism and Religious Indifferentism'. Freedom of conscience, Gregory stated, was a form of madness. In liberalism lay the rejection of supernatural revelation.

Pius IX

When Pius IX was elected Pope in 1846, he was initially hailed as a man who understood and sympathized with the social and political changes afoot in Europe. He played up to the image, freeing political prisoners and extending the franchise in the Papal States. But the revolutions of 1848 which swept through the capitals of Europe terrified him. He was forced to flee Rome when the Italian nationalist, Giuseppe Garibaldi, seized power there and declared it a republic.

The insurrection was short-lived. Pius was restored in 1850 by French troops, but returned with any liberal notions he had ever held gone. The movement towards a united Italy, growing in strength in the north of the country, was greeted with the Pope's intransigent hostility. Yet by 1860, his earthly domain had shrunk to little more than the city of Rome. With another wave of nationalist uprisings in 1870, it was swept away altogether.

Impotent to halt the political changes in Europe, Pius clung ever more tightly to his teaching authority to wreak a kind of revenge. Symbolic of the siege-mentality with which he infected the Catholic Church was his *Syllabus of Errors* of 1864, a condemnation of liberalism and the modern world in all its aspects. The climax of Pius's reign was the First Vatican Council, which gathered in Saint Peter's Basilica in December 1869 against a backdrop of Italian troops, finally claiming Rome as their national capital. It declared the papacy infallible in questions of faith and morality.

The intellectual siege was lifted to a degree with the election of Leo XIII (1878–1903). His encyclical *Rerum Novarum* of 1891, for example, belatedly engaged Catholics with the injustices created by industrialization. This was followed by the rise across Catholic Europe of Christian Democratic parties, with close links with the papacy, which had at their core the Catholic values set out in *Rerum Novarum*.

The rise of fascism

Catholicism failed to meet the challenge of new scientific thought in the nineteenth century, notably the work of Charles Darwin (1809–82) and his evolutionary view of humankind's origins. Instead Leo XIII retreated into a reaffirmation, in the encyclical *Aeterni Patris* (1879), of the enduring insights contained in the thirteenth-century teachings of Saint Thomas Aquinas. Modernism – both in the secular sense of the workings and concerns of the modern world, and in the Church sense of a progressive theological movement trying to engage with that world – was to be resisted at all costs.

The papacy remained neutral during World War I (1914–18), though Benedict XV (1914–22) made plain his opposition to, and pain at, the conflict. In its aftermath, the Christian Democratic parties of Catholic Europe did not prove sufficiently robust to counter the rise of fascism, especially in Italy and Germany. In Spain the Catholic Church sided instinctively with the fascist dictator, Franco.

The papacy was hindered in responding to these events on its doorstep in Italy by its 1929 concordat with the fascist leader, Mussolini, which had created the Vatican City State as the Pope's independent domain. In Germany, likewise, Catholicism struggled to provide an adequate opposition to Adolf Hitler. Though some local Catholic bishops and priests realized the danger that he posed, the overall view of the Vatican was that Hitler had to be endured as a bulwark against godless Soviet communism which posed the greatest threat of all to the future of Catholicism.

Pius XI (1922–39) realized the folly of this position in his 1937 encyclical, *Mit brennender Sorge* – the German phrase for 'With Great Anxiety'. It was a condemnation of Nazism and Hitler, whom it labelled 'a mad prophet possessed of repulsive arrogance'. Yet Pius died just as he was preparing another outspoken attack on the Nazi ideology. His successor, the wartime pope, Pius XII (1939–58), decided thereafter to say nothing, a silence on the subject of the Nazi Holocaust of 6 million Jews that has been much criticized subsequently.

Pius XII and wartime 'silence'

The principal charges against Pius XII were:

- that he made no public statement of condemnation even when he had firm evidence from 1940 onwards that the Nazis were exterminating millions of Jews
- that he was, therefore, anti-Semitic
- that he preferred to turn a blind eye to Nazi atrocities because he feared that Hitler was the only alternative to Soviet-style communism sweeping across Europe and destroying the Church
- that he believed the welfare of German Catholics was more important than that of Jews, and therefore was not willing to risk Nazi reprisals on Catholics if he spoke out
- that he only made some small and inconsistent gestures to help Jews after 1942 when it was clear Germany was facing defeat, and that his stance was therefore politically motivated not morally determined

- that Vatican diplomats failed to help Jews escape persecution by getting visas to travel to Palestine because the Pope opposed the idea of a Jewish homeland there
- that in the immediate post-war period, Pius showed his true colours by allowing the Vatican to be used as a conduit to spirit away Nazi war criminals to Africa and Latin America.

Defenders of Pius XII offer in his defence:

- that he was unaware of the true horror of the Holocaust
- that he believed he had to maintain a stance of strict neutrality in World War II so as to maintain the independence of the Church and play a part in the eventual peace settlement
- that he did make veiled references to the Holocaust in one broadcast; at Christmas, 1942, when he spoke out in general terms against 'progressive exterminations'
- that he worked behind the scenes with Church organizations to save as many as 5000 Jews living in Rome from deportation to the death camps
- that he intervened in March 1944 behind the scenes to pressure the Hungarian government to cease deportations of Jews which it agreed to in July 1944.

In response to the international attacks on Pius XII's record, the Vatican agreed in 1999 to establish a joint commission with Jewish historians to research its own archives and present a fuller picture of Pius's role. Two years later the Jewish members of the committee stood down in protest at Rome's refusal to open its archive fully. It said it couldn't because the sections in question hadn't yet been catalogued. Meanwhile the Vatican is pressing on with plans to declare Pius XII a saint.

Conclusion

The history of Catholicism can read as a history of the actions of popes. In part this happens because the greatest historical record is of the activities of the papacy rather than of individual Catholics. However, Catholicism is also a hierarchical organization, a system built in imitation of the Roman Empire. Indeed the Church replaced that Empire as the single greatest and most enduring political and moral force in Europe. So it is natural that any account of its history will be guided by the activities of its leaders.

Yet, as Catholicism entered the second half of the twentieth century, it was facing a new set of challenges – the unprecedented pace of social, scientific and economic change, a revolution in communications that meant its every action could be held up to scrutiny, and a much greater concentration on the rights of each individual. How it reacted has shaped the Catholic Church of today.

part three

the Catholic Church today

06
the modern Catholic Church

In this chapter you will learn:
- about the Second Vatican Council
- how the Church divided over contraception
- about the life and legacy of John Paul II.

To those who participated in or watched closely its discussions, the Second Vatican Council, which took place between 1962 and 1965, was an exhilarating, intoxicating time that shaped their faith and practice ever after. It was a reappraisal and reform of almost every significant aspect of the Church and its teaching – and this in an organization that says it never changes its mind. The decisions reached by the Council Fathers – the bishops from all around the world who met in Rome – have shaped Catholicism ever since in a direct and everyday way. Some have become so much a part of Catholic life that they go unquestioned, while others remain controversial and debated to this day.

Many Catholics, in the Council and post-Council era, have been forced to adjust from the moral certainties of old to a new world where there is not always a wholly satisfying answer to every question. Often there are many answers and Catholics have struggled to make sense of it all. The debate, discussion and dissent this has caused has, for many, been one of the great fruits of the Council, a Church engaged as never before at all levels in talking and praying about what it means to be a Catholic in the modern world. But others feel only pain at the divisions that have opened up and fear that in the rush to modernize, something essential may have been lost.

The Second Vatican Council

When Angelo Roncalli, the third of 13 children of peasant farmers from Bergamo, east of Milan, was elected as Pope John XXIII in 1958, he was regarded as a compromise candidate between those who wanted to continue Pius XII's legacy of standing resolutely apart from the modern world, and those who wanted change and engagement. Pope John was also seen, at the age of 76, as a 'caretaker pope', someone whose reign would be brief and who would pave the way for a younger successor.

Catholicism believes that when the cardinals of the Church gather to elect a new pope, they are guided by the Holy Spirit. It is how the Church explains some of the more unusual choices made in the line that is the Apostolic Succession. Certainly few expected that John XXIII, who had been a scholarly, popular but uncontroversial Patriarch (or Archbishop) of Venice before his election, would begin a Catholic revolution.

In person, he could not have been more different from the austere, unsmiling, careful Pius. John XXIII dispensed with protocol and mixed easily with the people of Rome, on visits to hospitals, to churches, to prisons and even walkabouts in the streets. Romans quickly took him to their hearts as 'good Pope John'; as did others.

He welcomed the leaders of other Christian churches to Rome as 'brothers' – including, in 1960, Dr Geoffrey Fisher, the Archbishop of Canterbury, the first Anglican leader to meet a pope since the Reformation. John abandoned Catholicism's instinctive hostility to communism, instead seeking ways of opening a dialogue with governments behind the Iron Curtain in a policy known as 'ostpolitik'. In January 1959, he surprised everyone by announcing plans to call what is now known to history as the Second Vatican Council, a gathering of the world's 3000 bishops in Rome, which would, as he put it, 'promote the unity of all Christian peoples'. It would, he said 'restore the simple and pure lines which the face of Jesus Christ's Church wore at its birth'. It would furthermore be an opportunity for *aggiornamento* – literally 'bringing up to date' – Catholicism with the modern world.

The Council opened on 11 October 1962 and lasted for four sessions, taking place in consecutive autumns through to 1965. It was enthusiastically reported to the world by the Church and secular press and by the international media, enthralled by the sight of such an unchanging institution as the Catholic Church gathering to reform itself.

Those in the Curia who regarded John's initiative with suspicion hoped to restrict the Council Fathers' remit, but the Pope did away with such caution when he told the assembled prelates, in his opening address, to fashion a new pastoral – or practical – approach rather than engage in sterile academic debate. There were ten commissions given the task of drafting documents in areas such as theology, liturgy and mission. These documents would then be debated by the whole Council, amended and finally approved. John moved decisively early on to remove obstacles to free discussion and gave his support to the bishops when they rejected the narrow guidelines laid down for draft documents by the Curia. A revolution was well underway by the time of John's death in June 1963. His successor, Paul VI (1963–78), enthusiastically continued his predecessor's work.

The key changes made

1 *Lumen Gentium* – The Dogmatic Constitution on the Church
  (November 1964) – reiterates traditional teaching that 'the
  sole Church of Christ which in the Creed we profess to be
  One, Holy, Catholic and Apostolic', is 'the Catholic Church,
  which is governed by the successor of Peter and by the
  bishops in communion with him', but it adds: 'Nevertheless,
  many elements of sanctification and of truth are found
  outside its visible confines.' One result is that when Anglicans
  convert to Catholicism today, they do not have to be
  baptized, since the Catholic Church recognizes their Anglican
  Baptism as valid. They are simply received into the Church.

2 *Lumen Gentium* also tackles how the Catholic Church sees
  itself and rejects the hierarchical model – with clergy making
  the rules and laity obeying them – in favour of a vision of the
  whole Church as 'the people of God', stressing the equality of
  vocation to the clerical and lay life, to priesthood and
  marriage, and setting out the principal role of those in high
  office in the Church as being that of service to fellow
  Catholics and to the world.

3 *Unitatis Redintegration* – The Decree of Ecumenism
  (November 1964) – sees the Council Fathers endorsing Pope
  John's support for the ecumenical movement from which
  Catholicism had previously stood apart. No longer was the
  goal to 'reconvert' Protestants to Catholicism, but rather the
  long-term aim of reunion of all separated brother and sister
  churches, to be achieved through dialogue and common
  prayer.

4 *Nostra Aetate* – The Declaration on The Relationship of the
  Church With Non-Christian Religions (October 1965) –
  stresses Catholicism's sincere reverence for other faiths such
  as Hinduism and Buddhism, its common ground with Islam,
  and its rejection of the accusation that the Jewish people can
  be blamed for the death of Jesus.

5 *Sacrosanctum Concilium* – The Constitution on the Sacred
  Liturgy (December 1963) – promotes the 'active
  participation' of the laity in the liturgy and concedes that
  parts of the Mass could henceforth be celebrated in the
  vernacular – i.e. in the local language – rather than Latin, as
  before.

6 In *Dei Verbum* – the Dogmatic Constitution on Divine
  Revelation (November 1965) – the Council Fathers
  encourage a much greater role for scripture in the life of the

Church, advocate the wider availability of the Bible in the 'mother tongues' of the faithful, and instruct both clergy *and* laity to undertake Bible study.

7 In *Christus Dominus* – The Decree on the Pastoral Office of Bishops in the Church (October 1965) – the Council holds up the example of the Apostles, working with their leader, Saint Peter, and orders that in all countries there should be a local bishops' conference able to make decisions on the application of the general teaching of Catholicism in the context of their areas. It promotes more international synods – or gatherings of bishops – as a way of encouraging greater co-operation throughout the global Catholic Church.

8 In *Gaudium et Spes* – The Pastoral Constitution on the Church in the Modern World (December 1965) – is embodied in the spirit of the whole Council, a desire to engage in a dialogue with the secular world.

Aftermath of the Council

The engagement with the world sought by the Council Fathers was given dramatic expression when Pope Paul VI began travelling to meet his global flock. For over 100 years popes had rarely strayed outside Rome and the Vatican. In 1964, Paul journeyed to Bombay to attend the Eucharistic Congress there, and in 1965 addressed the United Nations General Assembly to urge peace. He also renewed Catholicism's central administration, the Curia, in an effort to make it more outward-looking. In 1967, he established the Vatican's own Commission for Justice and Peace.

Such was the pace of change generated by the Second Vatican Council that many Catholics were not content, however, with the speed of the implementation of its various pronouncements. They believed that the spirit of the Council demanded that the overhaul of familiar teachings had to continue further into areas not dealt with by the Council Fathers.

There were others, coming from the opposite end of the spectrum of Catholic views, who were pressing Paul to use his authority to block some of the reforms proposed by the Council. Prominent among them was Archbishop Marcel Lefebvre (1905–91), a French Holy Ghost Father who had worked for most of his life in Senegal and West Africa. He engaged popular sympathy among some Catholics by his outspoken demand that the Mass must remain in Latin and the rite of the Council of Trent, rather than the updated, vernacular forms of the New Rite, introduced from 1970.

For many Catholics this change to the liturgy was the most contentious of the fruits of the Council. The distinguished Catholic historian, Christopher Dawson (1889–1970), summed up their distress when he wrote in opposition to what was called the Vernacular Movement: 'The existence of a common liturgical language of some kind is a sign of the Church's mission... to create a bond of unity between the peoples. The nations that are still divided from one another by the barriers of race and language leave their divisions and antipathies at the door of the Church and worship together in a tongue which belongs to none and yet which is common to all.'

However, Lefebvre's own rebellion went deeper. He rejected wholesale almost every aspect of the Council's work. For many years, the Vatican tried to reach some sort of accommodation with him and his small but dedicated band of followers, but when he began ordaining bishops who shared his views, and whom he intended would continue his work after his death, he was excommunicated in 1988. He died sometime afterwards, but in recent years there have been renewed efforts in the Vatican at reconciliation with those who followed him into schism.

Confusion and conflict

The majority of Catholics, however, were simply confused by what the changes would mean for their everyday lives and worship. Their parish churches, for instance, had to be reordered to accommodate the new-style liturgy, with the priest no longer standing at the altar with his back to the congregation. Priest and congregation were henceforth to participate together in the feast. So the altar rails, which had previously cordoned off the altar from the pews, were removed. And during Mass everyone was now expected to mingle and offer each other the 'Sign of Peace'.

Out, too, went time-honoured ceremonies and rites, while rephrasing ancient Latin into the vernacular allowed many to engage and participate more fully. Others, however, felt that something of the mystery and drama of the Catholic liturgy had been lost in translation.

The changes in the liturgy, however, encouraged hopes of still more change and reform. Two issues in particular dominated the decade after the Council. The first was the question of birth control. During the Council's debate on what was to become *Gaudium et Spes*, several of the bishops had urged the Catholic Church, as part of its engagement with the world, to re-examine its attitude to birth control. Catholic teaching was that only the so-called 'rhythm method' – abstinence during periods when conception was likely – was permissible, but it had a high failure rate, condemned Catholic couples to long periods without sexual relations, and moreover seemed to reinforce the idea that sex's primary purpose was procreation. With the liberation in attitudes to sex sweeping across Europe and the developed world in the 1960s, Catholicism was once again, its critics said, preaching ideals that were out of step with the reality of people's lives.

Part of that 1960s sexual revolution was the wide availability of the generally reliable oral contraceptive pill. It allowed women to take control of their own fertility for the first time. One of its inventors was an American Catholic obstetrician and gynaecologist, John Rock (1890–1984). He argued passionately in Church circles that it was a moral way of limiting the number of children a couple could produce.

Pope Paul referred the whole matter to a 64-strong commission of doctors, sociologists, population experts and theologians. It came back to him with two reports. The majority were in favour of reform. The minority – including some senior cardinals – opposed change. After much hesitation, Paul VI sided with the minority.

In July 1968, he published *Humanae Vitae* – On Human Life. His insistence that sex was something for heterosexual couples within marriage came as no surprise, but his demand that 'every marriage act must remain open to life' disappointed many Catholics who had already, in their own bedrooms, anticipated a change of heart and started to use contraception.

Linked with the dismay caused by *Humanae Vitae* and the Church's refusal to go with the times on the matter of contraception was a second broader issue. Many priests and religious people, swept up in the heady atmosphere of the aftermath of the Council and its challenging, unchartered decrees and constitutions, began to question and experiment in their ministry, claiming to be following the spirit of Vatican II. They took at face value the words in *Lumen Gentium* that 'the body of the faithful as a whole, anointed as they are by the Holy One, cannot err in matters of belief'.

This inevitably brought them into conflict with their local bishops. *Lumen Gentium* had also expressed the view that the Catholic Church must remain a hierarchical organization. In the ensuing battles, many priests and nuns ended up leaving the active ministry. Many of them married, no longer able to justify the demand that they remain celibate. Yet most also remained as devout and practising Catholics, part of the priesthood of the laity.

The disappointment caused by *Humanae Vitae* only increased this exodus. Some estimates put the number of priests worldwide who left the active ministry at 100,000. *Humanae Vitae,* moreover, caused a wider crisis of authority in Catholicism. In his novel *How Far Can You Go?,* the British writer, David Lodge, at the time a practising Catholic with a young family, summed up the impact of *Humanae Vitae* on his and many others' faith. 'If a Catholic couple decided, privately and with a conscience, to use contraceptives, there was nothing that priest, bishop or pope could do to stop them... Thus contraception was the issue on which many lay Catholics first attained moral autonomy, rid themselves of superstition, and ceased to regard their religion as, in the moral sphere, an encyclopedic rule-book in which a clear answer was to be found to every possible question of conduct.'

Until the Second Vatican Council, Catholics had, in public at least, felt bound in most circumstances by the decisions handed down by the papacy. The Council inspired them to trust in their own moral judgements. Now over possibly the most intimate and important decision they could make – how many children to have – *Humanae Vitae* seemed to force them to conclude that all the Council's talk of clergy and laity acting as one counted for nothing. Here was the Church reverting to type and imposing its wishes – in this case an all-male hierarchy insisting on its right to regulate a woman's fertility.

Yet it had no effective sanction. No one could punish Catholic couples for having fewer children. No one but the couple could know what went on in their bedroom. Even if the use of the pill or condoms was admitted in the confessional, most priests would grant absolution and the couple could carry on as before. It was a watershed in the moral authority of the papacy and the *magisterium* of the Church.

John Paul II

The last years of Paul VI's papacy saw a draining away of the enthusiasm unleashed by the Council, both in the Pope himself and within Catholicism. In its place came confusion as to what it meant to be a Catholic. Paul himself retreated ever more into the Vatican and died there, after a long illness. He was followed briefly by John Paul I (26 August–28 September 1978). Albino Luciani, another former Patriarch of Venice, died after just 33 days in office. Rumours he had been murdered were later conclusively refuted.

At the second conclave in a year, the cardinals unexpectedly chose Karol Wojtyla, the Cardinal Archbishop of Krakow in Poland. As a young bishop, he had participated in the Second Vatican Council and, it was hoped, would be able to sort out its legacy.

A papacy of firsts

Pope John Paul II (1978–2005) was:

- the first non-Italian to lead the Catholic Church for 455 years
- the first Slav to sit on the throne of Saint Peter
- the youngest holder of the office, at 58, for 130 years
- the first pontiff to travel the globe
- the first pope since the Reformation to visit Britain
- the first bishop of Rome since Saint Peter to visit the Rome synagogue
- the creator of more new saints in 27 years than his predecessors in the previous 500
- the author of more encyclicals and letters than any recent pope.

John Paul II's attitude to the fundamental changes within Catholicism that followed the Second Vatican Council was a complicated one. There were regular suggestions that he wished to 'put the clock back', especially when in 1985 he called a Special Synod of the world's bishops to examine the Council's legacy 20 years after it had closed. But these were essentially misplaced. His true mission seems to have been to reflect and reach clarity on some of the matters that had become contentious and divisive in the rush to implement the Council's teachings.

John Paul epitomized both the socially radical aspect of Catholicism that puts a premium on the fight for social justice, *and* its traditional, unchanging stance in the face of a secular world where scientific developments are now transforming the way people live at ever-greater speed. So he was simultaneously a champion of the developing world, calling repeatedly for the cancellation of third-world debt, *and* an implacable opponent of demands to approve new developments in the field of human fertilization and embryology.

He also spoke out loudly and clearly in defence of a traditional Catholic code of sexual ethics that made no concessions to the late twentieth century. John Paul in one sense simply endorsed everything that Paul VI had said on the question, but he sharpened it to an extraordinary degree, refusing to give any ground to those Catholics who had ignored *Humanae Vitae's* teachings. Catholics who practised artificial birth control, he said in 1984, were 'denying the sovereignty of God', thus becoming, in effect, atheists.

While respectful of other religious traditions, and personally warm in his relationship with the leaders of other Churches, he would not countenance making the core compromises in Catholic doctrine that would be necessary to change the Inter-Church movement into something more than friendly exchanges of views.

Some of the ecumenical initiatives begun in the wake of the Council – and initially boosted by, for example, John Paul's visit in 1982 to Canterbury Cathedral, the seat of international Anglicanism – ground to a halt during his papacy over issues like ministry, Eucharist and authority. Catholicism still retains among its beliefs the 1896 encyclical, *Apostolicae Curae*, in which the Anglican priesthood is declared to be 'absolutely null and utterly void'. John Paul refused all urgings to rescind this document.

In the spirit of engaging with the modern world, John Paul made his hallmark his travelling. He was seen in the flesh by more people than any other pope in history. Even when ill health, brought on by Parkinson's disease (a diagnosis never formally confirmed by his doctors on account of the extreme secrecy that traditionally surrounds the health of the Pope in Catholicism) took its toll in his later years, John Paul continued to visit his far-flung flock. His aim in undertaking such a demanding itinerary was threefold:

1 to offer himself as a visible sign of the unity of the worldwide Catholic Church
2 to stake an unmistakable claim for the papacy to a place on the stage of world political dramas
3 to hammer home, in his homilies when on tour, a basic set of beliefs around which all Catholics could rally. Top of the list were opposition to artificial contraceptives, abortion and divorce.

He was successful in drawing crowds and in inspiring great love and admiration in his flock, but there is little evidence to show that, on the three issues he chose to emphasize above all others, he made significant inroads into changing behaviour and secular norms. So, for example, he attracted widespread admiration amongst young people, who travelled in their hundreds of thousands, if not millions, to attend his special Youth Services and Days of Prayer, but there is little evidence that they then heeded his advice to wait until marriage to have sex and never to use condoms.

It was John Paul's role in supporting and inspiring – and indeed funding via the Vatican – the free trade union movement Solidarity in his native Poland that was undoubtedly his most obvious legacy. On his first visit home as Pope, in June 1979, he stood before one million Poles in Victory Square, Warsaw, where a 60-foot-high cross had been specially erected. No communist country had seen anything like it before. Here was the modern papacy intervening in the politics of the modern world to champion the aspirations of a people forced to live under communism for 40 years.

He became, according to many seasoned observers, the spark from heaven that set off the revolutions that tore down the Iron Curtain, first in Poland and then throughout Eastern Europe. And in keeping with his rejection of war as a legitimate means to settle humankind's disagreements, it was all largely done without violence – history's first great 'spiritual revolution'. The Kremlin grew to fear and loathe him so much, the Soviet leader Mikhail Gorbachev later tacitly admitted, that the KGB had some involvement in the 1981 assassination attempt on John Paul's life in Saint Peter's Square.

John Paul's slow, drawn-out death, never hiding from his flock and the cameras as his once-athletic body was ravaged by Parkinson's disease, showed his profound courage and a strong sense of divinely-ordained mission. However, by 2005, at the end of one of the longest pontificates in history, there were many Catholics – including senior cardinals – urging a change of direction from his successor.

Benedict XVI

The cardinals, elected Benedict XVI, John Paul's former trusted senior advisor. As Prefect (or head) of the Congregation for the Doctrine of the Faith, the German Benedict (then Cardinal Joseph Ratzinger) had been responsible for ensuring theological orthodoxy and silencing dissenters in the Catholic Church. He also enjoyed a reputation as being hard-line on many moral questions. In July 2003, for instance, he had labelled state recognition of homosexual partnerships as 'the legislation of evil'.

However, as Pope, Benedict has surprised. His strongest urge has been to shepherd all members of his sometimes fractured flock into a single corral. So his principal message has been one of reconciliation. Soon after he took office, for example, he lunched with the radical Swiss theologian, Father Hans Kung. Under John Paul II, Kung had been stripped of his licence to teach in Catholic universities, but here he was being invited back into the fold. And in his first encyclical, *Deus Caritas Est* (God is Love), published in December 2005, Benedict reflected on the importance of love in a poetic, positive and inclusive document.

There has been nuance in his theological statements, even if the language he uses is more open to a general audience than recent papal documents. He has also demonstrated a willingness to address difficult questions in relationships with other faiths – for instance, his controversial remarks on the history of Islam, made in 2006 on a visit to his native Germany. In general, he has seemed to want to avoid, at all costs, sounding too dogmatic.

Like John Paul, Benedict was also present at the Second Vatican Council, when he was a young priest, as *Peritus* (expert advisor) to Cardinal Joseph Frings of Cologne, one of the most outspoken reformers at the gathering. It clearly made an impact on him too – and continues to do so as he works to apply its thinking to the role of the Church in a changing world.

07

the hierarchy of Catholicism

In this chapter you will learn:
- how papal election methods have changed
- when popes can abdicate
- what a cardinal is.

Given how central the papacy is to Catholicism's distinctive identity and day-to-day operation, the method by which new popes emerge is of crucial importance. Saint Peter is said, in Catholic tradition, to have gathered an assembly of 24 priests and deacons and charged them with choosing his successor. The present method of election – by the College of Cardinals – is loosely modelled on this. In between times, however, a variety of other alternatives has been tried. It was only in the mid-twelfth century that Catholicism definitively restricted the vote to its principal clerics. In recent times there has been much talk of reforming the system, even involving the laity, but such changes as have been made have concerned small details.

How popes used to be elected

During the first millennium of Catholicism, new popes emerged in a variety of ways:

- by election by assemblies of the clergy and people of Rome
- by popular acclamation at the funerals of their predecessors
- from amongst the small circle of deacons who had served the previous pope
- by being imposed by local noble families in Rome
- on the orders of kings, emperors and princes who regarded the papacy as in their gift.

At a synod in the Lateran in 1059, however, Pope Nicholas II (1058–61) took the first steps towards the system that exists today. Henceforth the electors would be the seven cardinal bishops of Rome, he decreed, with the city's cardinal deacons, and then the people and ordinary clergy only included in the final stage to give their assent.

The reform remained contested for the next 100 years, not least by European monarchs who felt strongly that their views should be given precedence. And putative popes would still spend great sums on gifts for the Roman populace to win their assent. In the mid-twelfth century, however, the right of cardinals to be the sole electors was finally established by the Church. A two-thirds majority was required from 1179 onwards.

Who becomes a cardinal?

The word cardinal is thought to derive from the Latin for a hinge or a joint. It was a title first given to the priests around the ninth century, and was linked closely with the five great basilicas of Rome. One theory is that the word was chosen because these 'cardinals' were seen as hinges or intermediaries between the papacy, which controlled the five basilicas (Saint John Lateran, Saint Peter's, Saint Lawrence-outside-the-walls, Saint Mary Major, and Saint Paul-outside-the-walls) and the people of Rome.

In the eleventh century, the title had lost much of its original meaning by the time the cardinals were given control over the election of the Pope, and later over the Church in the inter-regnum between the death of one pope and the election of his successor. Yet a vestige of it remains to this day, with all cardinals of the Catholic Church having a 'titular parish church' in Rome under their protection.

The cardinals were described by Peter Damian (1007–72), the monastic leader and Church reformer, as 'the spiritual senators of the Roman Church' and they took on a relationship in regard of the papacy that had once been enjoyed by the great patriarchs of Constantinople, Jerusalem, Alexandria and Antioch, of key counsellors with a degree of independence, able in theory to rein in the papacy. They became effectively the senior management team of the Church, meeting with the Pope and each other, hearing legal cases and debating doctrine.

The term 'Curia', or 'court', used to describe cardinals and their assistants engaged in Rome in the Church bureaucracy, was first introduced by Urban II (1088–99) as he sought to reform the papal household. The cardinals' management of the Church's finances in particular, was later to be one of the major grievances of the Protestant reformers. At the time of the death of Leo X in 1521, when Martin Luther was facing the Diet of Worms, it was said that there were more than 2150 posts in the Curia, which could be bought, up to and including the role of the cardinal who was papal chamberlain.

From the twelfth century onwards, there were cardinals based in European cities other than Rome. Some of them – like Nicholas Breakspear, the future Hadrian IV (1154–9), the only English pope – served as legates, travelling to encourage Catholicism around Europe and impose the Pope's wishes. Others, like Cardinals Wolsey and Pole in sixteenth-century England, and Richelieu and Mazarin in seventeenth-century France, were powerful government ministers.

The cardinals' collective strength in the decision-making of the Church has always depended on their relationship with the reigning Pope. If he is strong, they are usually weak, and vice-versa. Popes have unfettered power to name cardinals, but the men they choose do not always do as their patron would wish.

Since 1630 cardinals of the Catholic Church have been given the title 'Eminence'. By tradition they wear scarlet. When chosen, it is often said that they have been 'given a red hat' by the Pope, though the colour is seen on them more often in the form of a scarlet skullcap, scarlet piping on their black cassocks, a scarlet belt (or *fascia*) and a scarlet cape (*ferraiolo*). Each cardinal is given a gold ring by the pontiff to symbolize their bond.

Papal conclaves

After a three-year hiatus from 1268 to 1271 in choosing a successor to Clement IV, new rules were introduced. The cardinal electors were to be held *cum clave* – literally under lock and key – until they could reach a decision. Locking the door was designed to focus their minds. It was even suggested that if they took more than three days, their food should be rationed, but this was later abandoned. The idea of the conclave was, however, established.

Numbers of cardinal electors remained, at 30, small throughout the mediaeval and Renaissance periods. To counter a subsequent growth, Pope Sixtus V (1585–90) introduced a limit of 70. This remained in place until the times of John XXIII and the Second Vatican Council, when John sought to include a greater variety of voices in subsequent conclaves. He did, however, enter new restrictions. He barred laymen who had previously been able, in rare cases, to be cardinals. All holders of a red hat must now be clergy.

Paul VI was reported to be considering a reform of the electoral process to reflect the spirit of the Council – possibly giving a greater role to the heads of local bishops' conferences – but the only change he actually delivered was to exclude from voting those cardinals who had reached the age of 80. Pope John Paul II made further minor changes in 1996, on the occasion of the opening of a new accommodation block to house the cardinals during their deliberations.

How popes are elected now

Those cardinals aged under 80 on the day of the previous pope's death gather in the Sistine Chapel shortly after his funeral. They are sworn to secrecy over their deliberations on pain of excommunication. They cast a series of secret ballots, two each morning, and two each afternoon. Potential candidates are identified as 'papabile' – capable of being Pope. If no verdict has been reached before nightfall, they go to the new Saint Martha's Hostel alongside the Sistine Chapel to sleep, and then start again the next day. (In past conclaves, they had been put up in a variety of small side rooms and broom cupboards around the chapel during the conclave. There was a fear that the new more spacious quarters would increase the length of their deliberations, but with the rapid election of Benedict XVI in 2005 it seemed, if anything, to have had the opposite effect.)

Cardinals cast their votes by writing in their chosen name on a piece of paper printed with the words *'Eligo in summum pontificem'* – 'I elect as Supreme Pontiff'. These papers are placed in a chalice on the altar underneath Michelangelo's 'Last Judgement'. Catholicism believes that the cardinals will be guided not only by their assessment of the needs of the Church in making their choices, but also by the Holy Spirit.

To be elected a candidate requires a two-thirds majority. In 1996, however, Pope John Paul II changed the rules so that if, after an agreed period of time, the cardinals so wish it, they can opt for a simple absolute majority of 50 per cent plus one.

If the ballot has proved inconclusive, the ballot papers are threaded together and burnt, producing a grey smoke that can be seen rising out of a chimney on the roof of the Sistine Chapel by onlookers. Once a verdict has been reached, however, a chemical is added to the ballot papers (it used to be wet straw) as they are put in the flames to turn the smoke white and so alert the world to the election of a new pope. Since 2005, it has also been decreed that the bells of Saint Peter's will ring, to clear up any debate in the square outside about what colour the smoke is.

Once chosen, the successful candidate puts on the white cassock of the Pope (three are set aside before the conclave, in small, medium and large sizes to cover all eventualities) and is led to the papal balcony, high above Saint Peter's Square, by the Dean of the College of Cardinals. He emerges onto the balcony and declares to the waiting crowd *'Habemus papam'* – 'We have a pope.'

In the past 200 years, no conclave has lasted over five days. Throughout the history of the papacy, 79 per cent of popes chosen have been Italians, 38 per cent Romans. In the nineteenth century, all popes came from the Papal States. However, with the election of first a Pole at the end of the twentieth century, and then a German in 2005, there is believed to be no obstacle now within Catholicism to a pope from anywhere around the globe. With a larger than ever proportion of the cardinal electors coming from the developing world, it is thought only a matter of time before one of their number becomes Pope and a symbol of a truly universal Church.

Can popes abdicate?

The papacy is traditionally a role in which the incumbent continues until he dies. However, during the long final illness of Pope John Paul II, as he struggled with the debilitating effects of Parkinson's disease, it was said that he did consider the question of abdication, but finally ruled it out, believing that if God wished him to relinquish the post, he would hasten his death.

Abdication is, however, specifically allowed for in Canon Law. As long as the decision is 'made freely and properly manifested', it states, the abdication does not need to be 'accepted by anyone'. Since the Pope is supreme governor of the Church, it is hard to know to whom he would deliver his abdication letter.

There were examples in the Early Church of popes who abdicated in circumstances that have been lost to history. Two later examples stand out: Pope Benedict IX (1033–44) abdicated in order to do penance as a monk for his sinful ways, but within two years was trying forcibly to reclaim the papacy. John Paul II is reported to have been worried about the effect of having two living popes in the Church if he were to abdicate. And Pope Celestine V, elected in 1294 after two yearss deadlock, was said to have been chosen on account of his blameless life as a monk-hermit. But that lifestyle left him ill-equipped to deal with the demands made on a pope, as he realized quickly. He was also 85. So, six months later, he published a decree allowing papal abdication which he then took advantage of. Not all approved of his decision. His contemporary, the great Italian poet, Dante (1265–1321), placed Celestine in the first circle of Hell in his *Inferno* for his 'great refusal'. Meanwhile Celestine's successor, fearful that he might become a rallying point for those disgruntled with the papacy, had him imprisoned until his death.

Papal infallibility

The claim to supreme, God-given authority has often been made by and of popes down the ages, implicitly, if not explicitly. Their teachings could not, it was said, be judged by anyone. The tradition that the See of Peter had preserved apostolic truth had clearly become enshrined by 519 when Pope Hormisdas (514–23) produced his 'Formula of Hormisdas', agreed by the Emperor Justin (450–527), citing Jesus's words to Peter in Matthew's gospel, entrusting him with leadership of the Church and endorsing the primacy of the see of Rome in which the Catholic faith was preserved in its purity.

However, the word infallibility was rarely used. Instead the concept was more that the office of pope, taken over many years, if not centuries, could not err. It was part of the Catholic reliance on the tradition of the Church carrying equal weight with the scriptures. No such claim was made, though, for individual holders of the papal office. Indeed, one of the reasons for the push to build greater co-operation between popes and the cardinals and councils of the Church was precisely so that individual popes could avoid, or be helped/forced to avoid, errors. The teaching might then be right, even if the teacher himself was wrong.

Yet during the schism of the late-fourteenth and early-fifteenth centuries, with different popes and their backers competing with the cardinals for authority in Catholicism, all sides began to make claims to speak infallibly or, more to the point, claims that their opponents were all too fallible.

The debate on infallibility was reignited in the nineteenth century, with traditional Catholic thinkers arguing that, in post French Revolutionary Europe, the papacy should be the blueprint for all restored monarchies, and that the power of individual popes to speak without error should therefore be publicly acknowledged. This recourse to supreme papal authority – known as 'Ultramontanism' – grew stronger as the century progressed with liberal revolutions that saw the political authority of the popes eroded as Italy moved towards reunification.

The issue was debated at the First Vatican Council, summoned by Pius IX in 1869. Few Catholics in the nineteenth century rejected out of hand the notion that the Pope might speak infallibly. The question was how, if at all, that should be defined. A minority felt the moment was inopportune to make such a statement when the whole of Europe was demanding greater democracy and freedom. When these opponents quoted the traditions of the Church, Pius IX is reported to have replied: 'I am the tradition.'

The Pope's wishes swung the vote, but limits were imposed. The text agreed by the cardinals, known as 'The Roman Pontiff', read: '... when he speaks *ex cathedra* ['from his throne'], that is, when, exercising the office of pastor and teacher of all Christians, he defines... a doctrine concerning faith and morals to be held by the whole Church, through the divine assistance promised to him in Saint Peter, is possessed of that infallibility with which the Divine Redeemer wished his Church to be endowed... and therefore such definitions of the Roman Pontiff are irreformable of themselves, and not from the consent of the Church.'

Routine papal teaching is not therefore infallible. The Pope has to be speaking in a particular and solemn form. No mention is made as to how such a definition should be arrived at – by the Pope acting on his own, or in consultation with his cardinals. These restrictions have meant that since 1870 only one papal statement has been deemed 'infallible' – the definition of the Virgin Mary's assumption, body *and* soul into heaven, made in 1950.

The Vatican

The central administration of the Catholic Church is known variously as the Curia, the Holy See and the Vatican. The last comes from the geographical area where it is located. The land to the west of the river Tiber where the Vatican now stands was an ancient pagan shrine that became, around the time of Jesus, a Roman pleasure garden. It was here that Saint Peter was executed in AD 64.

When Christianity achieved official recognition in the Roman Empire in the fourth century, a basilica was built in memory of Saint Peter, and a century later a papal palace was added. In the ninth century, Pope Leo IV (847–55) built walls around what became known as the 'Leonine City' to protect Saint Peter's from attack by Rome's opponents. He was prompted to act when raiders had emptied Saint Peter's tomb and scattered his bones.

However, until the fourteenth century popes did not reside in the Vatican. They lived at the Lateran Palace in the heart of the city of Rome, next to the Basilica of Saint John Lateran, the mother church of Rome. When they returned from exile in Avignon at the end of the fourteenth century, the Lateran Palace had fallen into disrepair and so popes made their home in either the Vatican or the Quirinale Palace.

When Italian forces took over Rome in 1870, the Quirinale was seized and later was to become the official residence of the Italian president. Pope Pius IX retreated into the Vatican, vowing never to come out again until his sovereignty was restored. In 1929 the Italian government, under Benito Mussolini, resolved what had become an embarrassing impasse by coming to an agreement with Pope Pius XI (1922–39) which created the Vatican City State as a *new* sovereign country – i.e. not a restoration of the Papal States – ruled over by the Bishop of Rome.

At 108 acres, it is the smallest sovereign state in the world and is largely enclosed by the Leonine Walls, and their subsequent extensions, and by the River Tiber. Several other sites on Italian territory were granted to the new state, including the papal summer palace outside Rome at Castel Gandolfo, and the other four great basilicas of the city. As well as a tiny railway station of its own, a heliport and a Post Office issuing its own stamps, the Vatican boasts its own radio station. Vatican Radio broadcasts to the world, putting across a distinctively Catholic message. Its daily newspaper, *L'Osservatore Romano* contains full details of all papal visits, meetings and pronouncements. It also has its own police force in the colourfully-dressed Swiss Guards. A force of Catholic Swiss troops has served popes since Julius II (1503–13). Their blue, red, orange and yellow ceremonial outfit is said to have been designed by Michelangelo but there is no evidence for this.

Most of the Vatican's territory, plus various outbuildings in Rome treated as Vatican sovereign territory, are used to house the Curia, the central bureaucracy of the Church, headed by senior churchmen but also employing significant numbers of lay men and women in the ranks. The principal departments of the curia are:

- the Secretariat of State (effectively the Vatican's Foreign Ministry, dealing with other governments)

- the Congregation for the Doctrine of the Faith (once the Holy Office in charge of the Inquisition, now concerned with discipline and theological orthodoxy)
- the Congregation for the Causes of Saints (in charge of the process for making saints)
- the Congregation for Catholic Education (overseeing seminaries and Catholic educational institutions)
- the Congregation for Bishops (in charge of appointing and monitoring bishops).

There are also the various courts and tribunals of the Sacred Roman Rota which interpret questions of Canon Law; the Vatican Bank, officially known as the Institute for Works of Religion and a source of great scandal in the 1980s because of its links with disgraced financiers; the Vatican's celebrated museums; and its equally renowned library, including the Secret Archive. The resident population of the Vatican City State is around 900.

Conclusion

No other leader of a world religion retains his own sovereign country. The existence of the Vatican City State gives the Catholic Church a place by right at many international gatherings and organizations. Because the Pope does not have to worry about the effect of his remarks, actions or teachings on any secular 'host government', he is in theory free to do and speak as he sees right. However, the reality is that the Vatican City State is entirely dependent on Italy to function – in terms of water, electricity, gas, transport etc. – and that relationship with Italy remains a sensitive and sometimes fraught one.

08

the Church on the ground

In this chapter you will learn:
- why priests are different from laymen
- about the vocations crisis
- where married men can be priests.

For many Catholics, the Vatican can seem a very long way away – geographically and spiritually. Even with the tireless travelling regime undertaken by Pope John Paul II – he visited 130 countries in all, with pictures of him kissing airport tarmac among the most familiar of his pontificate – the worldwide Catholic Church still remains a far-flung body. John Paul and his successor, Benedict XVI, have changed the composition of the College of Cardinals to bring in more figures from the developing world. However, the leadership and decision-making establishment of Catholicism still remains disproportionately European in make-up.

For Catholics in the developing world, then, and indeed for many Catholics in the developed world, their routine interaction with the hierarchy of their Church is through the local bishop, and most of all through the local priest.

The episcopate

The word bishop comes from the Greek *episkopos* or 'overseer'. Bishops are referred to by this term in the New Testament, though not in the gospels. Sometimes, however, the word is translated as 'elder'. So in Saint Paul's First Letter to Timothy (3:2), he sets out the appropriate qualifications to become a bishop or elder. The man must be of '…impeccable character. He must not have been married more than once, and he must be temperate, discreet and courteous, hospitable and a good teacher'.

As the Early Church developed, the term 'elder' dropped out of use and was replaced by bishop. A bishop would often be the leader of the Christians in major towns or cities, a pattern maintained to this day. From the second century onwards, as set out in the writings of key figures such as Clement of Alexandria (150–211), the task of ordaining priests was reserved to bishops. Where it is possible today, a bishop also bestows the sacrament of Confirmation on one of his regular visits to the parishes of his diocese. It is also the role of the bishop, each Maundy Thursday (immediately before the Easter celebration), to anoint sacred oils at the mass of chrism in the diocesan cathedral. This practice follows the traditions of anointing described in the Old Testament, as the sacred oils are then used by priests and the bishop in bestowing the sacraments of baptism, confirmation, holy orders and of the sick as will be described in a later chapter.

Throughout the history of Catholicism, bishops have filled many high political offices, but the 1983 *Code of Canon Law* expressly forbids it. In the wake of the Second Vatican Council, all bishops were required to join together into national bishops' conferences. CELAM, the Latin American and Caribbean Bishops' organization, is one of the largest examples of this in the world. It has its own secretariat. One of the bishops will be chosen as president, and others will take on specific responsibilities for areas of interest, such as liturgy, education, international development and so forth.

Bishops are appointed by the Vatican's Congregation for Bishops, taking advice from the Papal Nuncio (or ambassador) resident in the country in question. When a vacancy arises, he will produce, on the basis of his soundings with local Catholics and their leaders, a *terna* or list of three possible candidates. The final decision belongs to Rome, which has the right to reject the *terna,* ask for another, or simply pick its own candidates.

Bishops have to tender their resignation to the Pope at the age of 75, but in some circumstances are allowed to stay on longer. The colour worn by Catholic bishops is traditionally purple. Their garb includes a pointed hat (mitre), a shepherd's staff (crozier) and a pectoral cross, worn around their necks.

There are several types of bishops within Catholicism:

- Archbishops head major dioceses and act as 'metropolitan' or overseers of neighbouring dioceses.
- Suffragan bishops, or Ordinaries, are the heads of the individual dioceses that make up each metropolitan area or archdiocese.
- Auxiliary bishops are often appointed in large dioceses, to assist the bishop or archbishop, especially if he has other roles in the Church such as cardinal or member of a key Vatican commission.
- Titular bishops do not head real dioceses. Their title is derived from an ancient and now lost diocese of the Church. They will usually work in the Curia.
- Coadjutor bishops are appointed by the Vatican to assist existing bishops in their diocese, especially if the latter is in ill-health, and will succeed when the existing bishop stands down.
- Bishops Emeritus are retired bishops who often continue to serve in their diocese.

The nature of priesthood

To become a Catholic priest, you have to be male and willing to live a celibate life after ordination. For much of the twentieth century, a traditional regime existed whereby those wanting to be priests would, from the age of 11 or 12, enter first a Junior Seminary and then move straight on to studies for the priesthood at the Major (adult) Seminary, often taken in conjunction with a degree.

However, in recent years, reacting to the large numbers who subsequently left the priesthood because they felt they made a lifetime's commitment before they were mature enough to do so conclusively, candidates now more usually join once they have left secondary school, and often university. Many seminaries, especially in the developed world, encourage those who feel they have a vocation to go and see something of life before finally committing themselves.

Study for the priesthood is undertaken in a seminary, either in the local diocese, under the control of the local bishop, or elsewhere. Some candidates, especially those considered to have great academic potential, are sent to study in Rome. The basic training takes six years and includes time spent in parishes and learning by working alongside older priests. Many go on to take further qualifications once a bishop has ordained them.

Today Catholicism talks of priesthood in relation to both the laity and the clergy. All are seen as having a vocation because all are called to be Christians. So, in that sense, all believers are priests. In *Apostolicam Actuositatem* – the Second Vatican Council's Decree on the Apostolate of the Laity, issued in November 1965 – this concept was set out: 'There is a diversity of ministry [amongst Catholics] but a oneness of mission. Christ conferred on the Apostles and their successors the duty of teaching, sanctifying, and ruling in his name and power. But the laity likewise share in the priestly, prophetic, and royal office of Christ and therefore have their own share in the mission of the whole people of God in the Church and in the world.'

But modern Catholicism also makes a crucial distinction. Some are called to be ordained priests. 'The ministerial priesthood differs in essence from the common priesthood of the faithful,' states the *Catechism of the Catholic Church*, 'because it confers a sacred power for the service of the faithful. The ordained ministers exercise their service for the People of God by teaching, divine worship and pastoral governance.'

This harks back to the spirit of what had been up to then the practice of the Catholic Church, namely placing priests on a higher level than the laity. However, such a set-up was emphatically rejected at the Second Vatican Council. Both roles were seen as on a par, different but complimentary. In practice, however, many lay people continue to experience the Church as a hierarchical and clerical-dominated organization. For example, despite moves to encourage lay participation in the liturgy, many bishops in recent times have issued instructions curtailing the growing habit of having lay people preach at Mass. And Pope John Paul II was a firm believer in priests wearing their distinctive black cassock as they went about daily life rather than the same clothes as the laity.

The more profound question of priestly identity continues to concern the Church. To put it simply, is the priest a social worker who says prayers? Catholicism responds that the priest is distinct from the layman in that he is both icon and leader of the community. The second description comes in part from the priest's role in the parish, and from the freedom to act in a leadership role that his celibate state should afford him by removing other commitments and demands on his time.

But it also draws on the first part of the answer – namely that he is an icon. This means that Catholicism believes the priest stands in the place of Jesus, not just during the Mass when, at the consecration he turns the bread and wine into the body and blood of Christ, as Jesus did at the Last Supper, but also in other aspects of his life and activities, particularly with regard to the Church's social mission. 'Through the ordained ministry, especially that of bishops and priests,' states the *Catechism of the Catholic Church*, 'the presence of Christ as head of the Church is made visible in the midst of the community of believers.'

Although Catholicism places the vocations of the laity and the priesthood on an equal footing, it discourages those who have been ordained from seeking to return to lay status. There is a bureaucratic process, administered by Rome and called laicisation, but under Pope John Paul II it more or less ground to a halt. In the *Catechism of the Catholic Church*, it is written: 'It is true that someone validly ordained can, for grave reasons, be discharged from the obligations and functions linked to ordination, or can be forbidden to exercise them, but he cannot become a layman again in the strict sense, because the character imprinted by ordination is for ever. The vocation and mission received on the day of his ordination mark him permanently.'

Celibacy

The priesthood of the Catholic Church is reserved to celibate males. Catholicism is the only one of the Christian churches to insist upon this. Priests of the Orthodox tradition are permitted to marry, though only celibates fill the higher ranks of that Church. Martin Luther preached enthusiastically about the virtues of marriage for the clergy and followed his own advice with former nun, Katharina von Bora, who bore him six children.

For more than half of Catholicism's history, its priests were allowed to marry. Married men of proven virtue – *viri probati* – were prominent amongst the priests of the Early Church. It was only in 1139 at the Second Lateran Council that celibacy became mandatory. Some bishops did not enforce this ruling as forcefully as others and some married priests therefore continued into the sixteenth century when they were finally outlawed by the Council of Trent.

Today, then, those who feel a vocation to the priesthood are also required to have a second vocation – to celibacy. There were several reasons why the Church changed its position:

- The disreputable behaviour of some married priests who abandoned their wives, took lovers and tried to pass on Church property to their children.
- The contrast between such behaviour and the example of the lives of celibate monks, living in communities dedicated to prayer and service, making real in their own lives the separation described by writers such as Thomas Aquinas between the spiritual and the physical.
- The belief that a wife and children would inevitably distract a priest from his duties to his parishioners. Saint Paul wrote to the Corinthians (1:7:32), 'An unmarried man can devote himself to the Lord's affairs, all he has to worry about is pleasing the Lord.'
- The value placed on the celibate life as a 'sign of contradiction' in the secular world, a symbol of the rejection of that world's value system.

Most of these arguments relate to the practice of the Church, rather than directly to the scriptures. The celibacy rule is essentially based in the tradition of Catholicism. The one gospel passage quoted by those who support a celibate priesthood comes in Matthew, Chapter 19. Jesus has been approached by some Pharisees – members of a Jewish sect – who question him about whether a man can ever divorce his wife. 'What God has united,' Jesus replies, 'human beings must not divide.' Listening to the discussion, his disciples then said to him: 'If that is how things are between husband and wife, it is advisable not to marry.' But he [Jesus] replied, 'It is not everybody who can accept what I have said, but only those to whom it is granted. There are eunuchs born so from the mother's womb, there are eunuchs made so by human agency, and there are eunuchs who have made themselves so for the sake of the kingdom of heaven. Let anyone accept this who can.'

Matthew's words were quoted by Pope John Paul II in his 1979 *Letter to the Priests of the World* as a justification for continuing the rule of celibacy. It is, however, an interpretation that has been widely debated. What Jesus is really condemning, some theologians point out, is men who commit adultery. Moreover he seems to be responding to the suggestion from his disciples that if you have to be faithful to just one woman it is better not to marry at all, and therefore, by implication, to have several relationships. And it is important, the same theologians point out, to note Jesus's final words. 'Let anyone accept this who can.' Even if the official interpretation of the passage is correct, it should not then be made into a blanket rule in favour of a celibate priesthood.

Catholicism argues that there is further justification for the rule of celibacy to be found in Saint Paul's First Letter to the Corinthians. 'Yes, it is a good thing for a man not to touch a woman,' he writes (7:1–2). However, he goes on: 'Yet to avoid immortality every man should have his own wife and every woman her own husband... otherwise Satan may take advantage of any lack of self-control to put you to the test' (7:5).

It is not a conclusive endorsement of priestly celibacy. Saint Paul does not appear to have found marriage attractive for himself. He regarded it as a distraction from preparing for the Second Coming of Christ. Yet, neither did he condemn it in others. 'To the unmarried and to widows, I say: it is good for them to stay as they are, like me. But if they cannot exercise self-control, let them marry, since it is better to be married than to be burnt up' (I Corinthians 7: 6–9).

The Catholic Church, however, argues that the basis for priestly celibacy goes deeper than individual scriptural passages. It holds that the priest, at the altar, at the moment of consecration, stands in the place of Jesus at the Last Supper. And Jesus was, the gospels report, celibate and male. Hence the ordination of women cannot be considered.

While the celibacy rule is of relatively recent origin, the cult of virginity, in imitation of Christ, has been part of Catholicism from its earliest days. 'I consider there is nothing more calculated to cast a man's spirits down from the citadel,' wrote Saint Augustine in the fifth century, 'than the blandishments of a woman.' Saint Thomas Aquinas, writing in 1270 in *On The Perfection of Spiritual Life* appeared to agree: 'Among all human affection, the human spirit is especially held fast by married love... consequently the marriage bond is to be avoided at all costs by those tending to perfection.'

Today there are those who argue for a return to the earlier practice of married priests on the practical grounds of tackling the shortage of vocations in Catholicism, particularly in the developed world and Latin America. While vocations continue to rise in Africa and Asia, they are at a low ebb in Europe and the Americas. Latin American bishops, for instance, report that congregations may only see a Catholic priest once or twice a year because there are so few of them to go around.

Numbers of priests

The 2007 *Annuario Pontificio* – the official yearbook of the Vatican – which coves the period 2004 to 2005 reports the following statistics regarding the priesthood:

	No. of priests worldwide	No. of seminarians worldwide
2004	405,891	113,044
2005	406,411	114,439

There are, however, wide regional variations. Numbers of priests had grown in the period in Africa (3.8 per cent) and in Asia (3.55 per cent), but had fallen by 0.5 per cent in Europe and America. Similarly, numbers of candidates for the priesthood in Africa and Asia was increasing, but falling in Europe.

Research carried out by the University of Fordham in 2002 reported the following statistics for Catholicism in the United States:

	No. of priests	No. of seminarians	No. parishes without a resident priest
1930	27,000	16,300	0
1965	58,000	49,000	3 per cent
2002	45,000	4,700	15 per cent
2020*	31,000	N/A	25 per cent

*projected

Married priests

There is still a small number of married priests in the Catholic Church. Officially you can be both married and a priest if:

- you are a widower. It is not uncommon for a married man to choose to follow the path to ordination after the death of his wife
- you are a married ex-Anglican priest. Under Pope John Paul II, a special dispensation was allowed for the ordination of married, convert Anglicans who had joined the Catholic Church
- you are a member of one of the Eastern Rite Churches in communion with Rome.

To this official list might be added, unofficially, those men, ordained as Catholic priests, who have gone on to marry, but haven't applied for, or been granted laicisation, and who still regard themselves as priests.

Eastern Rite Catholic Churches

There are several Eastern Rite Catholic Churches, many based on the ancient Patriarchates of Alexandria, Antioch, Constantinople and Jerusalem, which have remained in full communion with Rome. Together they are believed to account for around 12 million Catholics worldwide. They have their own liturgical traditions and in most Churches priests can marry. The principal Eastern Rite Churches are:

- **The Armenian Catholic Church**: established in full communion with Rome by Pope Benedict XIV in 1742, a breakaway from the Armenian Apostolic (Orthodox) Church, which uses the Armenian rite, with principal centres in Armenia, Lebanon, Syria, Poland and the USA.
- **The Chaldean Catholic Church**: also known as the Chaldean Church of Babylon, and linked with Rome since the fifteenth century, after a split in the Assyrian Church of the East, but in full communion only since 1830. With 600,000 members in Iraq, Iran and Australia, headed by the Patriarch of Babylon of the Chaldeans who is also a cardinal.
- **The Coptic Catholic Church**: the result of a schism within the Coptic Orthodox Church, this 243,000-member Church is mainly based in Upper Egypt, uses the Alexandrian Rite and has been headed since 1895 by the Coptic Catholic Patriarch of Alexandria.

- **The Ethiopian Catholic Church**: developed out of a schism with the Ethiopian Orthodox Church, but distinct from Latin rite Churches in the region because its Ethiopic rite uses the ancient and otherwise little-used Semitic Ge'ez language. Less than one per cent of Ethiopians are members.
- **The Greek Catholic Church**: a group of closely related Churches spread throughout Eastern Europe and the Balkans using the Byzantine rite which split from Orthodoxy from the seventeenth century onwards.
- **The Maronite Church**: founded by the fifth-century monk and mystic, Saint Maron, who lived and died as a hermit on Mount Lebanon, this tradition within Catholicism numbers 3.5 million members worldwide, with 1.25 million forming a powerful Christian block in Lebanon.
- **The Melkite Catholic Church**: another Lebanese Eastern rite Church, linked with the other Greek Catholic Churches, using Arabic in the liturgy, with 1.3 million members.
- **The Syriac Catholic Church**: based in Syria, on the ancient patriarchate of Antioch, the result of a split in the Syriac Orthodox Church, but still using the same Antiochene rites.
- **The Syro-Malabar Catholic Church**: the largest of the Eastern rite Churches, with 3.8 million adherents, tracing their roots back to Saint Thomas the Apostle who, legend has it, arrived in India in 52 AD and was martyred in 72 AD.
- **The Syro-Malankara Catholic Church**: a break-away group of around 500,000 members from the Syro-Malabar Catholic Church.

Priestly titles

Most Catholic priests are known simply as 'Father'. 'Reverend' tends to be an Anglican form of address, though those Anglican priests who belong to the Anglo-Catholic tradition usually choose to be called Father.

There are two other titles used by Catholic priests: 'Monsignor' and 'Canon'. 'Monsignor' dates back to the fourteenth century and can be used for any high-ranking clergyman – a cardinal, archbishop or bishop as an alternative to other titles. When it is used of a priest, though, it denotes that he has been appointed by the Pope to one of three specific and honorary offices by way of recognition for his ministry:

1 Protonotary Apostolic (or honorary member of the Curia) which is restricted to priests over the age of 55 with more than 20 years since their ordination.
2 Prelate of Honour (to the Pope), restricted to those over 45 with 15 years' service.
3 Chaplain of Honour to the Pope, restricted to those over 35, with 10 years' service.

All appointments are usually made on the recommendation of the local bishop.

The second title of 'Canon' originally referred to those priests who lived next to or in the precinct of a cathedral and who played a role in its administration. This remains one reason for having the title Canon today, but there are two other types amongst the Catholic priesthood – those who belong to religious orders of canons (rather than brothers) and those who have been given the honorary title of Canon by the diocesan bishop in recognition of many years' service in a parish or elsewhere.

Religious life

Of the total number of Catholic priests in the world, it is estimated that some 65 per cent are 'diocesan' – i.e. working with their local bishop as part of the diocesan team, having trained in the diocesan seminary – and 35 per cent belong to religious orders. They may well be doing exactly the same work as diocesan priests, but owe their first allegiance to their order.

Religious orders have been part of Catholicism since the Desert Fathers of the third century. Members live in communities, based on the model of Jesus and his Apostles. If the first centuries of the Church were dominated by the prospect and, often, the reality of martyrdom, then, once the Roman Empire accepted Christianity, some felt the need to find new and radical ways to answer Jesus's call in baptism to lead pure lives. They found it in monasticism.

Saint Antony (251–356) is regarded by Catholicism as the founder of monasticism. He gathered other like-minded individuals to join loose-knit communities of hermits in the Egyptian desert. They would spend their time in prayer, study and hard labour, focusing on Jesus's example when he spent 40 days and 40 nights in the desert and, like him, resisting the temptations put in their path by the Devil.

They attracted many admirers, among them Benedict of Nursia (480–547). He was so appalled by the excesses of life in Rome, where he had been sent to study, that he lived first as a hermit and then within a community of monks. Around 529 he established the monastery at Monte Cassino, 80 miles south of Rome, and drew up his *Rule* – or guide to monastic living – which has become the bedrock of Western monasticism in the Catholic Church.

Excerpts from the Rule of St Benedict

1 The first degree of humility is obedience without delay. This is the virtue of those who hold nothing dearer to them than Christ; who, because of the holy service they have professed, and the fear of hell, and the glory of life everlasting, as soon as anything has been ordered by the Superior, receive it as a divine command and cannot suffer any delay in executing it.

2 Since the spirit of silence is so important, permission to speak should be rarely granted, even to perfect disciples, even though it be for good, holy, edifying conversation.

3 Let no one presume to give or receive anything without the Abbot's leave, or to have anything as his own since they are not permitted to have even their bodies or wills at their own disposal.

4 Then are they truly monastics when they live by the labour of their hands, as did our Fathers and the Apostles.

5 When we wish to suggest our wants to persons of high station, we do not presume to do so except with humility and reverence. How much the more, then, are complete humility and pure devotion necessary in supplicating the Lord who is God of the universe!

6 Let them sleep clothed and girded with belts and cords – but not with knives at their sides, lest they cut themselves in their sleep – and thus be always ready to rise without delay when the signal is given and hasten to be before one another at the word of God, yet with all gravity and decorum.

The religious charism

Not all members of religious orders are priests. Benedict wasn't, for example, and neither were those who, much later, joined the Congregation of Christian Brothers, founded in Ireland in the

1820s by Edmund Rice, and noted for their work in schools around the English-speaking world. But all members of religious orders do take vows of chastity, poverty and obedience, in imitation of Jesus. They live in a community, a community that is, in effect, their family.

All orders and congregations have what is known as a 'charism' – or unique aim – laid down by their founder. At the Second Vatican Council, they were told to return to those charisms, a process that saw many orders undergoing a major overhaul, changing their style of dress, their way of life and their work, for example, by withdrawing from running fee-paying schools or private hospitals in the developed world, and focusing instead on the unanswered needs of the marginalized in their own societies, or in the developing world.

Most of the religious orders of the Catholic Church will have at their core one of the following traditions:

- **Augustinian** There are today five main branches of the Augustinian family, following variations on *The Rule of Saint Augustine of Hippo*. Distinguishing characteristics include an emphasis on truth and learning ('Nothing conquers except truth and the victory of truth is love,' Augustine wrote), and on music ('To sing once is to pray twice' is another maxim of Augustine's). Augustinians have been heavily involved in missionary work and include both mendicant – i.e. rejecting property and living on charity – and lay branches. In the lay fraternities and societies (for women), individuals can live out the Augustinian rule as part of their daily secular lives.
- **Benedictine** Saint Benedict's *Rule* emphasizes peace, prayer, *lectio divina* (meditative reading) and work. It calls on monks to be part of 'a school for the Lord's service' and lays down key virtues of obedience to the abbot (or head of the community), and moderation. The various branches of the Benedictine family include both male and female groups, united under the Order of Saint Benedict, as well as independent orders following the Benedictine Rule such as the Congregation of Cluny, the Cistercians and the Trappists. There are also Anglican and Orthodox Orders of Saint Benedict.
- **Dominican** Growing out of the Augustinian Rule, the Dominicans – or Order of Preachers to give them their correct title – were founded in 1216 by Dominic de Guzman (1170–1221) in southern France. Dominic rejected the pomp and wealth of the papacy and insisted instead on 'zealous

speaking', 'apostolic humility' and 'austerity'. The combination of the active life – preaching the gospel – and the contemplative – study and prayer – is at the heart of the Dominican tradition. From originally staffing the Inquisition, the Dominicans are among Catholicism's foremost intellectuals. They eschew the large monasteries of other orders and are mendicants, relying on charitable hand-outs to fund their work.

- **Carmelite** The tradition of the Carmelites holds that their origins lay in a community of hermits founded in the twelfth century on Mount Carmel in Israel by Saint Bertold (d.1195), a former Crusader. Their rule stresses the central role of prayer and includes great Marian devotion. Many Carmelite communities are enclosed – shut off from the world and dedicated to silence, contemplation and prayer (often for the world). There are also active branches. Saint Teresa of Avila (1515–1582) led a successful reform of the order in the sixteenth century, returning it to its original charisms of poverty and rejection of worldly values and founding the Discalced Carmelites.

- **Franciscan** *The Rule of Saint Francis* of 1223 lies at the heart of the three modern branches of the Franciscan family. All follow the example of their founder, Saint Francis of Assisi (1181–1226), in embracing poverty so as to work with the most needy. Originally Saint Francis set up his Order of Friars Minor to mitigate the sufferings of the urban poor, feeling that the older religious orders in their grand monasteries had abandoned them. The Franciscans were traditionally fierce defenders of the papacy and staffed the Inquisition.

- **Jesuit** The Jesuits are today the largest male religious order in Catholicism with (in 2007) 19,216 members. They were founded in Paris in 1534 as the Company of Jesus by Ignatius Loyola, receiving papal approval at the Society of Jesus in 1540. Working in education, making converts and resisting the encroachments of Protestantism, the Jesuits had a quasi-military organization that earned them the title 'the foot soldiers of the Pope' in the Counter-Reformation years. They spread around the globe, being prominent in the missions. Their key text is Ignatius's *Spiritual Exercises*.

At different stages in Catholicism's history, religious orders have wielded great influence in the Church, but have also suffered periods of decline. There was, for example, a burst of growth in the mid-nineteenth century, with many orders founded to do apostolic work in schools, hospitals, and the overseas missions. In just three years, between 1862 and 1865, Pope Pius IX approved the establishment of 74 new religious orders for women.

Since the Second Vatican Council, with many orders struggling to reconcile their founding charism with their historic role, there has been a general exodus from the religious orders, especially in the developed world. Research from Fordham University on the situation in the USA gives a snapshot of the issues faced. In 1965, there were, it reports, 3559 Jesuit seminarians. By the year 2000 that figure had dropped to 389. In the Christian Brothers, the figures for the same period fall from 912 to just seven.

However, there has been a corresponding growth in the developing world. The religious orders see this as proof that their charisms still have great appeal for Catholics, though it is worth considering how far they are attracting recruits – as once they did in Europe – because they can offer young men and women who would otherwise go without an education the possibility of study in a secure and structured environment.

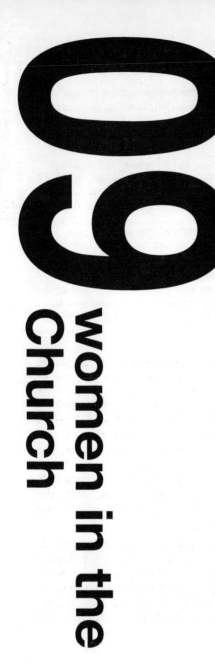

09
women in the
Church

In this chapter you will learn:
- about the role of nuns
- why women can't be priests
- of Catholicism's most celebrated nuns.

The attitude of Catholicism to women is often debated, principally because, by continuing to reserve the ordained ministry to men, the Church goes against secular trends to treat men and women as equal. Changing attitudes on women priests in other Christian Churches have further concentrated attention on this issue. In 1994 the Church of England decided to permit the ordination of women, and in 2006 the Episcopal (Anglican) Church in the USA elected its leader Bishop Katharine Jefferts Schori, who was raised a Catholic.

One of the features of Catholicism, however, is its reluctance to follow what the rest of the world is doing or thinking, and so it has rebutted forcibly the argument that it should grant absolute equality for men and women before God. Yes, the Catholic Church has said, men and women are equal, but they are also different. This view has been put forward with great persistence by recent popes, most notably John Paul II who had a great devotion to Mary, the mother of Jesus, and who often held her up as the supreme role model for women to follow.

Women priests

The Catholic Church teaches that women cannot be ordained as priests. 'I declare that the Church has no authority whatsoever to confer priestly ordination on women and that this judgement is to be definitively held by all the Church's faithful,' Pope John Paul II wrote in 1994 in *Ordinatio Sacerdotalis* (On Ordination to the Priesthood). The document was released under his ordinary *magisterium* – or teaching authority – so he was not speaking *ex cathedra* (from the throne), using his extraordinary magisterium, and so the teaching cannot be considered infallible under the terms agreed by the cardinals in 1870. However, the Vatican was anxious at the time to stress that this was a final and definitive statement on the matter.

It moved to discourage wider discussion of the matter. So when, in 1994, a British nun, Sister Lavinia Byrne, published *Women At The Altar*, a book on the history of female ministry in the Church, touching on the archaeological evidence for women priests in the Early Church, the Vatican insisted that official Church publishing houses withdrew the book. Byrne was later to leave her religious order.

Evidence for women priests in the Early Church

The evidence includes:

- inscriptions on mid-fifth-century tombstones in southern Italy and Calabria referring to presbiteras – or women priests
- a letter, written by Pope Gelasius I (492–6) to Catholics in southern Italy recounting reports of 'women officiating at sacred altars and all matters reserved for the male sex'
- fifth-century mosaics in the Ancient Roman Church of Saint Prassede, which stands on the site of one of the meeting places of the first Christians in the city, showing four women, one of whom is described as 'Theodora Episcopa' – 'Theodora, the woman bishop'
- in the Catacomb of Saint Priscilla in Rome, where first-century Christians hid from their Roman persecutors, is an early third-century fresco, showing seven figures, one, if not all of them women, celebrating the Eucharist by re-enacting the Last Supper.

The official reaction to such archaeological and historical evidence is to point out that Pope Gelasius was, in his letter, clearly intent on outlawing women priests in southern Italy, that Theodora was the mother of Pope Paschal I (817–24) and therefore was being called a bishop as a mark of respect to him, and that – in the words of the Vatican Commission on Sacred Archaeology – the fresco in the catacombs may show women at the Eucharist, but that it is a man (albeit in a veil) who is actually breaking the bread.

Objections to women priests

Catholicism's objections to women priests are that:

- Jesus chose only men as his Apostles
- the priest represents Jesus who was incarnated on earth as a man
- there is no tradition within the Church of women priests.

Some feminists have suggested that to this list might also be added that Catholicism regards women as second-class citizens, but Pope John Paul II was anxious to dispel any such impression. In his 1988 apostolic letter, *Mulieris Dignitatem* (On the Dignity of Women), for example, he wrote: 'The Church gives thanks for each and every woman: for mothers, for sisters, for wives, for women consecrated to God in virginity.' He argued that women were the equal of men, but different from them. 'In the name of liberation from male domination, women must not appropriate to themselves male characteristics contrary to their own feminine originality. There is a well-founded fear that if they take this path they will... deform and lose what constitutes this essential richness.'

In his 1995 *Letter to Women*, he emphasized women's role as mothers, bringing 'God's own smile upon the newborn child, the one who guides your child's first steps, who helps it to grow, and who is the anchor as the child makes its way along the journey of life.' He also applauded women who have careers and bemoaned the fact that for so long women had been 'relegated to the margins of society and even reduced to servitude'.

Those who argue in favour of women priests describe Jesus's decision only to choose male Apostles as dictated by the context of his times. Women were rarely seen in public roles in the society in which he lived. But in *Ordinatio Sacerdotalis*, John Paul II rejected this proposition, pointing out, had he wanted a female Apostle, he could have included his mother.

Repeatedly in their teachings, popes have used the Virgin Mary as a role model for women. While her virginity, even after giving birth, her freedom from the stain of original sin and her assumption body and soul into heaven may all set her apart from other women, Catholicism teaches that her example should guide and inspire her sex. In his 1995 *Letter to Women*, John Paul wrote:

> The Church sees in Mary the highest expression of the 'feminine genius' and she finds in her a source of constant inspiration. Mary called herself the 'handmaid of the Lord'. Through obedience to the word of God she accepted her lofty yet not easy vocation as wife and mother in the family of Nazareth. Putting herself at God's service, she also put herself at the service of others: a service of love. Precisely through this service Mary was able to experience in her life a mysterious, but authentic reign. It is not by chance that she is invoked as 'Queen of heaven and earth'. The entire community of believers thus invokes her; many nations and peoples call upon her as their 'Queen'. For her, 'to reign' is to serve! Her service is 'to reign'.

From 2004, a small group of American, German and South African Catholic women who wanted to be priests started to challenge the authorities. They were first ordained as priests by three male bishops, in good standing with the Vatican, and then three of these women were consecrated bishops. They have subsequently ordained a number of other Catholic women as priests. On several occasions the ordinations have taken place on a river boat, so as to avoid falling under the jurisdiction of the local Catholic bishop. The women argue that their ordination is legitimate because it is linked back to male bishops who are in their turn linked back through the Church to Saint Peter himself. The Vatican, however, has rejected this, saying that the three male bishops had no authority whatsoever to overturn the Pope's ruling and by doing so risk excommunication.

Nuns

The term 'nun' is associated in popular Western culture principally with Catholicism, though there are Anglican, Orthodox, Lutheran, Jain, Buddhist and Taoist nuns. In Catholicism, there is a distinction between a nun and a religious sister, though the terms are often used interchangeably, albeit sometimes inaccurately. In general, a nun has taken solemn vows and is usually a member of an order and often lives in an enclosed community. A religious sister, by contrast, will be a member of an Institute or Congregation of sisters, has taken simple vows, and usually is involved in practical work in the community. Benedictine nuns are traditionally known as Dames – the female equivalent of Dom, used for Benedictine monks – but this practice is now dying out.

In the decades since the Second Vatican Council, the number of nuns has dropped sharply throughout the Western world. According to a study by Fordham University, there has been a decline in the USA from a peak of 180,000 in 1965 to just 75,000 in 2002 and a projected 40,000 in 2020. Many of the smaller orders – particularly those founded to work in schools or hospitals in the eighteenth and nineteenth centuries – have now gone many years in developed countries without attracting any new vocations. Most, however, have also seen growth in numbers in the developing world and have progressively moved their centres of operations there.

Even the contemplative orders such as the Carmelites and Benedictines – traditionally more successful in attracting vocations in recent times – have seen numbers dwindle in the

West. Only the Missionaries of Charity, established in 1950 by the late Mother Teresa of Calcutta, with their distinctive blue and white habits, have seen a growth in vocations *all* around the globe.

To the vows of chastity, poverty and obedience, the Missionaries of Charity add a fourth – 'wholehearted and free service to the poorest of the poor'. With a rigid structure, and a great emphasis on prayer and active work, the order has little time for study or self.

Women dedicating their lives to prayer and service have been part of Christianity from the earliest of days. Saint Paul, writing to the Corinthians (I 7:34–35) urged unmarried women to devote themselves 'to the Lord's affairs; all she need worry about is being holy in body and spirit'.

By the third century, there is evidence of communities of women, turning their backs on sexual relations, and dedicating themselves to God. In the fourth century, the wealthy widow Saint Paula (347–404) established a communal house for women in Bethlehem, where they would offer a welcome to pilgrims to the city and cared for Saint Jerome who had settled nearby.

With the growth of monasticism in the West under Benedict and his followers, female monasteries were established where women would take vows of chastity, poverty and obedience and wear long, simple garments that covered their bodies, and a headdress or wimple over the head, leaving only their faces visible. Often both male and female houses would exist side-by-side, but separate, sometimes presided over by female abbesses like the renowned Hilda of Whitby (614–680).

Hilda was the great niece of a king. Other abbesses who enjoyed similar authority over men were often highborn, but the Church distrusted their independence. By the twelfth century, when Saints Francis and Dominic were establishing orders of travelling friars and preachers, efforts to set up the female equivalent, for instance by Saint Clare in 1215, were restricted by the demand from the papacy that the women should live under enclosure – within a convent – for their own safety. They were allowed to travel outside the walls, but this freedom was strictly curtailed in the centuries ahead.

It was not until the seventeenth century, in 1633, when the Sisters of Charity were established in France, that religious sisters were permitted to serve the community by living without enclosure. Another pioneer in this area was Mary Ward who founded the Institute of the Blessed Virgin Mary, a teaching order with a Jesuit style of spirituality. One of the few activities that could be carried out within the rules of enclosure had been teaching, and this was now able to spread outward throughout Catholicism. The tradition of nun teachers providing education to girls who would otherwise have no access to it goes back many centuries.

The enclosure did, however, have great appeal as a place of safety where women were permitted both to govern themselves and to study, something often denied them elsewhere. The experiment of Beguinage in the Low Countries in the thirteenth century, with houses of learning for religious women that were not enclosed, had struggled in the face of male hostility.

In the eighteenth and nineteenth centuries, the growth in the number of active female orders was rapid. Their decline in the twentieth century, however, was just as rapid. In the clerical-lay divide of Catholicism before the Second Vatican Council, nuns were classified as laity and were often expected to perform secondary, assistant roles to priests. Since the Council, though, they have been encouraged to modernize their dress and return to their founding charisms so as to reassess where they should be concentrating their work. There have been a number of high-profile appointments of religious sisters to senior positions within the Vatican Curia. However, worldwide, according to official statistics, the number of nuns continues to fall. In 2000 there were 801,185 compared to 968,526 in 1975.

Ten significant nuns

Blessed Teresa (1910–97): Known in her lifetime as Mother Teresa of Calcutta, this Albanian-born nun, trained in Ireland, was based in India from 1929, initially as a teacher with the Institute of the Blessed Virgin Mary. In 1946, she experienced 'a call within a call' to serve the poorest of the poor, those she identified as 'the hungry, the naked, the homeless, the crippled, the blind, the lepers, all those people who feel unwanted, unloved, uncared for throughout society, people that have become a burden to the society and are shunned by everyone'. In 1950 the Missionaries of Charity were given official approval and later a male branch was established. In 1979 Mother Teresa received the Nobel Peace Prize for her work, and by the time of her death there were 4000 sisters working in 123 countries. Pope John Paul II beatified her in 2002.

Saint Therese of Lisieux (1873–97): Known as 'the Little Flower', this French Carmelite is associated with the 'Little Way' approach to living out faith and spirituality which focuses on the importance of small deeds. 'Great deeds are forbidden me,' she wrote. 'The only way I can prove my love is by scattering flowers, and these flowers are every little sacrifice, every glance and word, and the doing of the least actions for love.' She suffered ill health throughout her life, which she bore gladly, dying at the age of 24. After her death, her spiritual journal, *The Story of a Soul* became a bestseller.

Mary Ward (1585–1645): The English founder of the Institute of the Blessed Virgin Mary, also known as the Loreto Sisters and today as the Congregation of Jesus, was regarded as too radical in her day. She tried contemplative life but preferred running a school for rich and poor girls in Saint Omer in France. Her efforts to set up an Institute without enclosure, obligation to attend choir, a habit or control by the local bishop, were controversial. Though her communities spread, they were suppressed by the papacy in 1630, only reviving 73 years later and growing into a force in the education of young women worldwide.

Saint Teresa of Avila (1515–82): A highborn Spaniard, she entered the Carmelites as a teenager, in the face of family opposition, but experienced long periods of ill health. She was also a mystic who saw visions – spiritual ecstasies – which led some to suspect she was possessed. With John of the Cross, she led a radical reform movement within the Carmelites, believing the order to have become too lax. Her work culminated in the establishment of the Discalced Carmelites – so called because they abandoned leather or wooden sandals and went barefoot.

Saint Catherine of Siena (1347–80): This Italian theologian and mystic rejected life in an enclosed convent to become a lay member of the Dominicans and to live, alone, as an anchoress in the world, dedicating herself to prayer, fasting and mortification of her flesh. In 1366 she had a vision which she described as a 'mystical marriage' with Jesus and thereafter dedicated herself to the service of the poorest. She had many subsequent visions and died, like Jesus, at the age of 33.

Mother Julian (1342–1416): This mediaeval mystic and spiritual writer from Norwich was a Benedictine nun who lived out her life an anchoress, walled into a cell in the city church of Saint Julian from which she took her name. Her *Revelation of Divine Love* is believed to be the first book written in English by a woman and contains the phrase that sums up her spiritual insight: 'All shall be well, and all shall be well, and all manner of things shall be well.'

Saint Elizabeth of Hungary (1207–31): One of the few female saints in Catholicism to have been married and to have had children, Elizabeth was a king's daughter who was betrothed at the age of four to Louis IV of Thuringia. Inspired by Francis of Assisi, she began doing charitable works, freed to act by her royal status. On the death of her husband when she was 20, she resisted attempts to force her to remarry and became a lay Franciscan, founding a hospital for the poor and sick.

Saint Clare of Assisi (1194–1253): Clare was one of the first followers of Francis of Assisi and, like him, embraced radical poverty as part of her commitment to the poor. She escaped from her family's demand that she should marry and founded a convent at San Damiano, following a Franciscan rule. Her sisters cut their hair short, wore rough tunics, but were unable to follow their male counterparts in travelling to tend the poor and sick, having, as women, to stay in the enclosure.

Saint Hildegard of Bingen (1098–1179): This remarkable German polymath gave her life to the Church from the age of eight, going on to found a monastery for women at Bingen on the Rhine. She composed music, wrote poems, theology and medical and botanical tracts.

Saint Hilda of Whitby (614–80): The royal-born Abbess was part of the tradition of Celtic monasticism which spread from Ireland, via Iona in Scotland, to the 'new' Christian lands of England. In 657 she founded a double monastery on the banks of the River Wear, with separate houses for men and women living out their beliefs in peace, charity and biblical study. Her reputation as a teacher led to the holding of the first synod of the English Church at Whitby in 664.

Consecrated virgins

From the earliest times of Christianity, according to Saint Paul, there were unmarried women and widows who consecrated their lives to God and to the service of others. In his First Letter to Timothy (5:9) Paul suggests that the widow 'can give herself up to God and consecrate all her days and nights to petitions and prayer. The one who thinks only of pleasure is already dead while she is still alive.'

However, this ancient practice fell into disuse with the rise of women's religious orders. The Second Vatican Council restored it. Since 1970 Catholicism has laid down once again a solemn rite in which women are, as the *Catechism of the Catholic Church* puts it, 'betrothed mystically to Christ'. The rite during which they make their pledge, which has to be performed by a bishop, describes the dedication of a woman's perpetual virginity as 'a transcendent sign of the Church's love for Christ'.

Some consecrated virgins form themselves into associations. Others use the freedom their choice has given them to live as hermits or solitaries. Some – like the art critic and popular religious broadcaster Sister Wendy Beckett – are also nuns, but live separately from the orders they originally joined.

Conclusion

Though the Second Vatican Council sought to abandon the distinction between clergy and laity, it remains one of the features of contemporary Catholicism. However, old barriers have gone and, with the decline in vocations, there is much more co-operation, even at the highest levels of the Catholic Church, than ever there was. Those who suggest that permitting the ordination of married men and women to the priesthood are, their critics say, missing the point. Not only would it go against the tradition of the Church, it would not reverse the fall in vocations. However, a contrary argument would question whether, when individuals be they celibate women, or married males and females, genuinely feel themselves called by God to a life of priestly service, that calling can be ruled unacceptable by the Catholic Church.

part four

teachings and traditions

10

the sacramental and devotional life of Catholics

In this chapter you will learn:
- about distinctive Catholic liturgical traditions
- about transubstantiation
- about fish on Fridays.

All faiths have their rites, rituals and distinctive and sometimes eye-catching devotions. Catholicism is no exception. At its heart is the Mass and the Eucharist – for Catholics literally the bread of life. The other sacraments play an important part, though some more so than others. And then there are devotions, some of long standing, rooted in the scriptures and the tradition of the Church. Not all have endured, and some have suffered a decline in popularity but are still associated in the public mind with Catholicism. Others have roots elsewhere but have become part of the fabric of Catholic life.

The Mass

The Catholic Church, instructs the *Catechism*, 'obliges the faithful to take part in the Divine Liturgy on Sundays'. This obligation can also be discharged by attending Mass on the evening of the previous day – i.e. the Saturday. Exceptions are made in cases of serious illness or of heavy child-care responsibilities, particularly of infants, but absence otherwise is regarded as a grave sin. Despite this, Mass-going statistics for many hitherto staunchly Catholic countries in the developed world (for example, Ireland), have shown a fall in recent years in the numbers attending every Sunday without fail. The growing tendency to interpret what had once been seen as hard-and-fast rules, highlighted earlier in the wake of the publication of *Humanae vitae*, seems to be having an effect in this area too.

Though the term 'Mass' to denote a standardized liturgy is believed to date back to the fifth century, there were Eucharistic celebrations recorded as early as the second century by Saint Justin Martyr (100–165).

> On the day we call the day of the sun, all who dwell in the city or country gather in the same place. The memoirs of the Apostles and the writings of the prophets are read, as much as time permits. When the reader has finished, he who presides over those gathered admonishes and challenges them to imitate these beautiful things. Then we all rise together and offer prayers for ourselves... and for all others, wherever they may be, so that we may be found righteous by our life and actions, and faithful to the commandments, so as to obtain eternal salvation.
>
> When the prayers are concluded, we exchange a kiss. Then someone brings bread and a cup of water and wine

mixed together to him who presides over the brethren. He takes them and offers praise and glory to the Father of the universe, through the name of the Son and of the Holy Spirit and for a considerable time he gives thanks that we have been judged worthy of these gifts.

When he has concluded these prayers and thanksgivings, all present give voice to an acclamation by saying: 'Amen'. When he who presides has given thanks and the people have responded, those whom we call deacons give to those present the 'eucharisted' bread, wine and water and take them to those who are absent.

Saint Justin Martyr to Emperor Antoninus Pius in 155

What the saint describes will be familiar to all Catholics as the structure of the modern Mass. It consists of readings from the Old and New Testaments, and then from the Gospels, a homily by the priest and intercessions – together known as the Liturgy of the Word – followed by the offering of gifts, the consecration of the bread and wine, the kiss of peace, and communion (the Liturgy of the Eucharist).

As a whole, the form of the Mass imitates Jesus at the Last Supper, walking around the table (the altar in the Mass) explaining to his Apostles the scriptures, then breaking bread with them. The priest stands in the place of Christ.

The participation of the laity (the congregation) has, however, been encouraged in recent years as readers, in the presentation of the offerings at the Offertory and as ministers of the Eucharist, assisting the priest in the distribution of the bread and wine, the body and blood of Christ. There have also been limits maintained on such participation. Only the priest, for instance, can read the gospel and, while lay members of the congregation can speak from the pulpit after the communion, the homily is usually reserved for priests.

The Eucharist

Catholics are obliged to receive the Eucharist at least once a year, if possible during the Easter season. Attendance at first the Sacrament of Reconciliation and then at the Eucharist is traditionally referred to as 'Easter duties'. The Catholic Church does not allow members of other faiths to receive communion at its Eucharistic celebrations (and discourages Catholics from doing so at those of other Christian denominations) because it holds that their understanding of Christ's real presence in the bread and wine is different from that in Catholicism.

'The mode of Christ's presence under the Eucharistic species is unique,' the *Catechism* instructs. 'It raises the Eucharist above all the sacraments as the perfection of the spiritual life and the end to which all the sacraments tend.' Catholics believe that contained in the consecrated bread and wine is the body and blood of Christ, as well as his soul and divinity, 'truly, really and substantially'.

This belief is called transubstantiation and was an issue in the Reformation debates, and remains a key point of divergence in the talks going on under the auspices of ARCIC – the Anglican Roman Catholic International Commission. Other Christian faiths tend to emphasize the symbolic nature of the bread and wine in the Eucharist. Catholicism goes considerably further. 'It is,' the *Catechism* points out, 'presence in the fullest sense: that is to say, it is a substantial presence by which Christ, God and man, makes himself wholly and entirely present.'

The consecration as part of the Eucharist acts as a potent reminder of God's ability to transform everything. 'Be convinced,' wrote Saint Ambrose (338–97), Bishop of Milan and one of the most influential Early Church Fathers, 'that this is not what nature has formed, but what the blessing has consecrated. The power of the blessing prevails over that of nature because, by the blessing, nature is changed.'

In the Eucharist, Catholicism believes, Christ is wholly and entirely present among the faithful. By receiving the unleavened bread or host, the bond with Jesus is strengthened. In John's Gospel (6:55–7), Jesus tells those who doubt him: '... anyone who does eat my flesh and drink my blood has eternal life, and I shall raise him up on the last day. For my flesh is real food, and my blood is real drink. He who eats my flesh and drinks my blood lives in me and I live in him.'

Baptism

Catholics are encouraged to have their children baptized as soon as possible after birth. In the past this would have meant within a few days, but now it can be months. The Church used to teach that unbaptized children who died in infancy would spend eternal life in Limbo, a place of 'natural happiness' but away from the presence of God. The Vatican formally abandoned this concept in 2005, dismissing it as a hypothesis.

In baptism, Catholics are cleansed by water of the stain of original sin – the legacy to humanity of Adam and Eve's disobedience in the Garden of Eden – and become members of the Church. Baptism, from the Greek word meaning to plunge or immerse, has been part of the Church from its earliest days. Jesus was baptized by his cousin, John the Baptist, and Saint Peter, in the Acts of the Apostles (2:38), made his first conversions, following Jesus's death, resurrection and ascension into heaven, with the words 'every one of you must be baptized in the name of Jesus Christ for the forgiveness of all your sins and you will receive the gift of the Holy Spirit.'

These words remain at the core of Catholicism's understanding of baptism. Part of the celebration of the sacrament is a form of exorcism. Either the adult to be baptized or the parents and godparents on behalf of an infant will formally reject Satan and all his ways. There will also be an anointing with chrism, or sacred oil, consecrated by a bishop, signifying the gift of the Holy Spirit. Infants will be wrapped in a white garment, symbolizing that they have 'put on Christ', as Saint Paul describes it in his Letter to the Galatians (3:27), and a candle, lit from the Easter candle, signifies that Christ, the light of the world, has entered the newly baptized.

Adults who wish to be baptized as Catholics have first to undertake the distinct steps set out in the Rite of Christian Initiation of Adults. These preparations can take up to 12 months. Those who have already been baptized as Anglicans are not required to undergo a second baptism. After a period of instruction, they are received into the Catholic Church.

Reconciliation

Also known as penance or confession or the sacrament of conversion, reconciliation allows Catholics to confess their sins to a priest and receive absolution. Sins can be either 'mortal' – the more serious – or 'venial' – the everyday. Confession of venial sins is recommended but not obligatory. Confession of mortal sins is required of Catholics in order to prepare them to receive the Eucharist.

Catholicism teaches that only God has the power to forgive sins, but the priest acts in his place. Penitents may be asked to say a penance – usually made up of several prayers – and/or occasionally to undertake works for the poor and needy. They also have to promise to do their best to avoid sinning again.

There are different permitted formats for the sacrament. Traditionally it has taken place in a confessional box, with the priest and penitent separated by a grille and curtain, going through a set series of prayers and responses. In more recent times, there has been a move to more informal face-to-face conversations.

The Catholic Church regards anything said during the sacrament of reconciliation as private. The phrase 'the seal of the confessional' expresses the belief that what is said during the sacrament cannot be repeated elsewhere. Even if a murderer has confessed, the priest cannot reveal his identity to the authorities. The priest can refuse absolution and is required to if he does not believe that there exists true contrition – described by the Church as being in mind *and* heart, and accompanied by sorrow for the deed or sin itself.

A priest may also, before granting absolution, require some other form of reparation other than the saying of prayers. In rare cases this may include contacting the relevant civil authorities if, for instance, a murderer is confessing.

Many dioceses have what are described as 'reserved sins' where a priest needs special permission from his bishop to grant absolution. These vary but can include abortion, murder or child abuse. If the priest does not have permission, the penitent must be referred to the local bishop.

Catholicism also allows for penance to take place within communal celebrations – with participants preparing themselves together and then giving thanks for the forgiveness they receive. The personal confession of sins and individual absolution are included within a liturgy of readings, an examination of conscience, and a communal request for forgiveness. Though such rites of general absolution were introduced into Catholicism in 1975, the Vatican has stressed repeatedly that they should only be used sparingly or in exceptional circumstances.

First Holy Communion

First Holy Communion is one of the landmarks of any Catholic's life. Traditionally girls will wear a white dress (to symbolize purity) for their first reception of the sacrament of Eucharist, though this has been discouraged in more recent times, with the Church anxious to concentrate candidates' minds on what is happening rather than how they are dressed.

In the earliest times of the Church, it was common for very small children to participate in the Eucharist from the time of their baptism. This is still the practice in some of the Eastern rite Churches in communion with Rome. However, for most Catholics, since the Council of Tours in 813, First Holy Communion comes at around the age of seven or eight. This is when the child is judged capable of fuller participation in the sacramental life of the Church.

Preparation, by lay catechists (or teachers) is usually done in conjunction with that for first reconciliation. There has been some dispute over the centuries over this close connection between the two sacraments, with a body of opinion holding that, while it is possible for a child of eight to be sufficiently mature to receive the sacrament of penance, Eucharist should be delayed until the early teens because of its central importance in Catholic life. The Vatican has repeatedly rejected this argument.

Confirmation

Confirmation is regarded in Catholicism as an opportunity to mark an increase and deepening of God's grace, originally bestowed by baptism. It is an occasion when the presence in each individual of the Holy Spirit, first marked at baptism, is confirmed and the seven gifts of the spirit are bestowed to guide individuals through their adult lives.

The seven gifts of the Holy Spirit are based on an Old Testament passage (Isaiah 11:2–3) and have been defined by, amongst others, Saint Thomas Aquinas in his *Summa Theologica*. They are:

- wisdom
- knowledge
- counsel (also known as right judgement)
- fortitude (courage)
- understanding (common sense)
- piety
- fear of the Lord (wonder and awe in God).

Aquinas wrote that the first four concern the intellect and the remaining three the will towards God.

Confirmation is sometimes known as 'the sacrament of Christian maturity' and usually takes place when a young Catholic has reached the age of discretion in their early teens – though some Catholic dioceses have pioneered programmes where Confirmation follows hard on the heels of First Holy Communion.

Confirmation is usually administered by the local bishop. Candidates, having completed a lengthy preparation, will each have a sponsor. The bishop will anoint the candidate's forehead with sacred chrism and say the words 'Be sealed with the gift of the Holy Spirit.' Traditionally candidates also choose a saint as their patron.

Marriage

The Catholic Church teaches that God instituted marriage. He created Adam and Eve, a man and a woman, out of love and called them to love each other. Marriage was the expression given to that love and God was part of the partnership.

The symbolism of marriage pervades Catholicism. The covenant between God and the people of Israel in the Old Testament is presented, for example, as a nuptial bond. Jesus performs his first miracle at a wedding feast in Cana, and nuns are often described as 'brides of Christ'.

Jesus mentions marriage explicitly in the gospels and his injunction against divorce is clear and remains strong in Catholic teaching. Catholicism does not, as a rule, permit second marriages, unless either one original spouse has died or the first marriage has been subjected to the annulment procedure (which will be discussed in a later chapter). Catholicism does not recognize divorce and those who do divorce, in the civil courts, and then remarry are, as a rule, unable to receive the Eucharist. In very rare circumstances, priests may agree to bless second marriages and waive the bar on going to communion.

The *Catechism* makes it plain that marriage is to be preferred to remaining single. Marriage, it states, is the antidote to 'self-absorption, egoism, pursuit of one's own pleasure, and [an opportunity] to open oneself to the other, to mutual aid and to self-giving'. Catholicism also teaches that marriage is the proper context for sex and for the bringing up of children.

When two Catholics marry, it is usual for the sacrament to be bestowed within a Nuptial Mass. The Church requires that they give their free consent. Traditionally, it has frowned on mixed marriages, requiring Catholics who marry non-Catholics to marry quietly and without great ceremony. This, however, is rarely the case today. The current *Catechism* restricts itself to pointing out the potential pitfalls of 'disunity' in the marital home. It does, however, reiterate the practice of requiring the Catholic partner to a marriage to pledge to have any children of that marriage baptized and educated as Catholics. This is now more often expressed as a hope than as a demand.

Holy Orders

The sacrament of Holy Orders is the means by which Catholicism passes on to a new generation the original mission entrusted by Jesus to his Apostles. The word 'Orders' comes from the Roman term for a governing body. Hence ordination is the ceremony by which you join the governing body.

There are three degrees of the sacrament – the episcopate, the presbyterate and the diaconate (or bishops, priests and deacons). Bishops, the Church teaches, enjoy the fullest expression of the sacrament. Priests are their co-workers, but deacons exist to serve and assist. They are ministers but not priests. Often candidates for the priesthood will first be ordained as deacons, but since the Second Vatican Council, the Catholic Church has brought back the permanent diaconate, opening it to married men, to create a group who can assist the priesthood with the distribution of Holy Communion, preaching, and presiding at funerals. There is a growing demand amongst those who support women's ordination for the permanent diaconate to be opened to women as a first step in answering the vocation many women feel they have.

Only bishops, as the successors of the Apostles, can confer the sacrament of Holy Orders. Since the Second Vatican Council, those who have received it are referred to as the ministerial priesthood to distinguish it from the common priesthood of the faithful.

The sacrament of the anointing of the sick

Once popularly known as extreme unction, this sacrament was usually associated with anointing the dying, but today it aims to bring comfort and healing to anyone who is sick. It was recommended to all the faithful and was instituted, Catholicism teaches, by James, the Apostle and brother of Jesus. It follows time-honoured rituals in older faiths of the anointing of the sick with oils.

Today's sacrament, as set out by the Vatican in the Apostolic Constitution, *Sacram unctionem infirmorum*, issued by Pope Paul VI in 1972, consists of the anointing of seriously ill people on the forehead and hands with blessed oil made from olives and other plants. 'Through this holy anointing,' the priest or bishop says, 'may the Lord in his love and mercy help you with the grace of the Holy Spirit. May the Lord who frees you from sin save you and raise you up.' If the person recovers and then falls ill again at a later point, he or she can receive the sacrament more than once.

Other devotions

Outside of the sacraments, there is a variety of other devotions which have long been a part of Catholic life. Some are seen both inside and outside the Mass – for instance making the sign of the cross as you enter a Catholic Church with holy water from a stoup near the entrance. This is a form of cleansing and reminds Catholics of the baptismal vows. It is usual to genuflect – go down on one knee and make the sign of the cross – before the main altar of the church and the tabernacle, which contains the Blessed Sacrament. Most Catholic churches will house a place where visitors can light candles as part of seeking God's help for themselves or others who are sick or who have died. These banks of candles are usually found in front of a statue of the Virgin Mary who intercedes with God on behalf of humanity.

As well as these devotions there are a number that take the form of rituals outside the Mass.

The Rosary

The word 'rosary' refers to both a set of devotional prayers, and the beads which are traditionally used while reciting those prayers. Rosary beads, as they are often called, have been in existence since at least the twelfth century. In 1166 Saint Rosalia, a descendant of Charlemagne who lived a hermit's life of prayer and fasting, was buried with a Rosary in her hands. Modern sets of rosary beads consist of a string of 50 beads, gathered in groups of ten (decades). The beads are used to count off the prayers as a Catholic says the Rosary.

Each decade of the Rosary consists of one 'Our Father', ten 'Hail Marys' and one 'Glory Be To the Father'. While reciting these prayers, either out loud or, more unusually, silently, Catholics are directed to meditate and reflect on three sets of mysteries – the Joyful, the Sorrowful and the Glorious. To these three, in 2002, Pope John Paul added an optional fourth – the Luminous. Each of the sets of mysteries consists in five themes, one for each decade as you go around the rosary beads.

The Joyful mysteries

1 The Annunciation – when the Angel Gabriel came down to earth to tell Mary that she was to give birth to God's son.
2 The Visitation – when Mary's elderly, childless cousin Elizabeth visited her and shared Mary's news, as well as announcing her own miraculous pregnancy with the child who was to become John The Baptist.
3 The Nativity – the story of Jesus's birth in a stable.
4 The Presentation of Jesus at the Temple – when Jesus, still a small child, was taken by his parents, as Jewish law required, to be presented at the Temple in Jerusalem and was greeted, according to Luke's gospel (2:22:40) by Simeon who hailed him as the Messiah in a prayer known today in Catholicism as the *Nunc Dimittis*.
5 The Finding of Jesus in the Temple – another episode recounted only by Luke (2:41–50) when the 12-year-old Jesus accompanies his mother and father to the Temple, falls into conversation with the elders, and is believed lost by his distraught parents.

The Sorrowful mysteries

1 The Agony in the Garden – Jesus's torment in the Garden of Gethsemane before he is betrayed by Judas and arrested.
2 The Scourging at the Pillar – when Jesus is whipped on the orders of Pontius Pilate, the Roman governor.
3 The Crowning With Thorns – when his captors torment Jesus on account of his claim to kingship and place a crown of thorns on his head.
4 The Carrying of the Cross – the *via dolorosa* – or way of sorrow – that was Jesus's climb to the hill of Calvary.
5 The Crucifixion.

The Glorious mysteries

1 The Resurrection.
2 The Ascension – of Jesus into heaven.
3 The Descent of the Holy Spirit – giving the Apostles courage after their leader had finally left them.
4 Ascension of Mary – body and soul into heaven.
5 The Crowning of the Blessed Virgin Mary – as queen of heaven.

The Luminous mysteries

1 The Baptism of Jesus in the River Jordan – by his cousin John the Baptist.
2 The Wedding Feast of Cana – Jesus's first miracle, where he turned water into wine.
3 Jesus's Proclamation of the Kingdom of God – a phrase that occurs in the New Testament almost 100 times.
4 The Transfiguration – when Jesus goes up on a mountain and meets Moses and Elijah, the only Old Testament figures described as already in heaven, and is greeted by God as his son.
5 The Institution of the Eucharist – at the Last Supper.

The Rosary remains a popular devotion and many parish churches will set aside a time or times in the weekly calendar when Catholics can gather there to say the Rosary together. Acknowledging a decline in interest in the Rosary in younger Catholics, Pope John Paul II, in 2002 in *Rosarium Virginis Mariae*, urged all, especially families, to return to this devotion:

The Rosary of the Virgin Mary, which gradually took form in the second millennium under the guidance of the Spirit of God, is a prayer loved by countless saints and encouraged by the magisterium. Simple yet profound, it still remains, at the dawn of this third millennium, a prayer of great significance, destined to bring forth a harvest of holiness. It blends easily into the spiritual journey of the Christian life, which, after 2000 years, has lost none of the freshness of its beginnings and feels drawn by the Spirit of God to 'set out into the deep' in order once more to proclaim, and even cry out, before the world that Jesus Christ is Lord and Saviour, 'the way, and the truth and the life', 'the goal of human history and the point on which the desires of history and civilization turn'.

Benediction and Exposition of the Blessed Sacrament

On its own, the word 'Benediction' is simply a plea for divine help, based on Jewish practice, but the form of Benediction most often seen in Catholicism is Benediction of the Blessed Sacrament. This devotion, which dates back to the thirteenth century, involves the host being displayed on the altar in an elaborate monstrance – or container. The congregation sings and prays, both silently and together. They are, Catholicism teaches, in the real presence of Christ, found in the host, his body. The priest may also, as part of Benediction, process around the church, wrapped in a humeral veil or shawl, and holding the monstrance, surrounded by incense (fragrant smoke). Many of the hymns and prayers that are part of Benediction will make reference to the Virgin Mary. A popular one is 'O Salutaris Hostia'.

Like the Rosary, Benediction has declined in popularity but remains part of the weekly calendar of many parish churches. An alternative is Exposition of the Blessed Sacrament, often scheduled before or after the Mass. 'The Catholic Church,' states the *Catechism*, 'has always offered and still offers to the sacrament of Eucharist the cult of adoration, not only during Mass, but also outside of it, reserving the consecrated hosts with the utmost care, exposing them to the solemn veneration of the faithful, and carrying them in procession.' From earliest times, Catholics have been encouraged to pray before the consecrated

host, either placed on the altar in a monstrance, or seen through
the open doors of the tabernacle.

The Angelus

A short traditional devotion, accompanied by the ringing of a
bell, to recall Christ's incarnation as a human being, the Angelus
remains part of the national culture of countries such as Italy
and Ireland. In Italy, the main state television channel
broadcasts the Pope saying the Angelus each Sunday at noon,
while in Ireland both the state radio and TV channels include it
in their daily schedules.

It takes its name from the opening line – *Angelus Domini
nuntiavit Mariae* ('The Angel of the Lord declared unto Mary')
– and consists of a series of statements and replies, followed by
the recitation of the Hail Mary. Its origins are disputed but are
believed to lie in eleventh-century monasticism where three Hail
Marys would be said during the ringing of the evening bell. Its
format was standardized in the seventeenth century.
Traditionally it is recited three times a day – at 6.00 a.m., at
noon, and at 6.00 p.m.

Stations of the Cross

A ritual of prayer, readings and reflection, the Stations of the
Cross recalls the final hours, or Passion, of Jesus Christ. It can
take place outside – most notably around the Coliseum in Rome
on Good Friday during the pontificate of Pope John Paul II –
with worshippers moving between 14 depictions of Christ's final
suffering and death. Since the times of Saint Francis of Assisi,
who encouraged the practice, most Catholic churches will also
include depictions of the 14 stations. It is most popular in the
season of Lent, especially on Good Friday, the day when
Christians believe Jesus was crucified.

The 14 stations are:

• Jesus is condemned to death
• Jesus receives the cross
• Jesus falls the first time
• Jesus meets his mother
• Simon of Cyrene carries the cross
• Saint Veronica wipes Jesus's face with her veil

- Jesus falls the second time
- Jesus meets the women of Jerusalem
- Jesus falls the third time
- Jesus is stripped of his garments
- Crucifixion: Jesus is nailed to the cross
- Jesus dies on the cross
- Jesus's body is removed from the cross
- Jesus is laid in the tomb.

There is a body of opinion within Catholicism that argues that a fifteenth station should be added – commemorating Jesus's resurrection.

The Divine Office

Based on the Jewish habit of praying at set hours of the day and night, the Divine Office was taken up by the Apostles and by the fourth century had become part of Catholic life, especially for priests and monks. It was considered too burdensome for the laity – requiring reading in a time of widespread illiteracy – and they were directed instead towards the Rosary. But the Second Vatican Council urged the benefits on the Divine Office on all Catholics.

Traditionally the Divine Office divided the day into eight distinct times for prayer, reading and reflection known as the canonical hours:

1 Matins – usually in the middle of the night
2 Lauds – at dawn
3 Prime – at 6 a.m.
4 Terce – at 9 a.m.
5 Sext – at midday
6 None – at 3 p.m.
7 Vespers – in the evening
8 Compline – night prayer before going to bed

The Second Vatican Council, however, reduced the list from eight to seven by incorporating Prime with Lauds.

At each of these stages of the day and night, Catholics turn to their breviary – a book of readings from the Bible, with particular emphasis on the Book of Psalms, prayers and chants. In some monastic communities, the Divine Office also includes singing.

Fasting and abstinence

Catholicism has fewer dietary laws than many other faiths. The best known of its practices is that of eating only fish on Fridays. This was always a misrepresentation of the Church's position. Catholicism has long urged all members, over the age of 14, to treat Fridays (except when they are Solemnities – feast days such as the Annunciation, the Assumption or All Saints' Day) as days of abstinence. On such days, they should avoid eating meat. In the past it was assumed that fish was the only alternative, but there are many dishes that can be eaten without meat in them.

These days of abstinence are designed to afford Catholics an opportunity to atone for their sins, and to reflect on the sacrifice of Jesus on Good Friday by making a small sacrifice of their own.

Until 1966, the laws of abstinence were strictly followed. However, in that year Pope Paul VI issued new guidelines, maintaining the practice, but devolving responsibility for who should take part and how other devotions might be substituted for abstinence, to local bishops' conference and to Catholics' own consciences. In some countries, Catholics are encouraged to find time on Fridays to offer some sort of support to the needy in their community rather than abstain from meat.

Separate from the days of abstinence are periods of fasting where no food or drink is to be taken. These apply to all Catholics aged between 18 and 60 and require them on two days in the year – Good Friday and Ash Wednesday (the first day of the penitential season of Lent) – to fast by only having one meal a day (or two small meals). Previously Catholics had treated the whole season of Lent, and often Advent (running up to Christmas) as times of fasting.

Today there is a much greater emphasis on the individual to renounce an aspect of their daily life, which they chose as a way of marking Lent. Any money saved by this is then given to charity. But abstinence and fasting still has a place, according to Pope Paul VI in his 1966 Apostolic Constitution, *Paenitemini* ('On Penance'). 'Mortification aims at the liberation of man, who often finds himself, because of concupiscence, almost chained by his own senses. Through "corporal fasting" man regains strength, and the wound inflicted on the dignity of our nature by intemperance is cured by the medicine of a salutary abstinence.'

There are older traditions of fasting in Catholicism. Many used to fast and do penance on the Ember Days – four sets of three days (usually a Wednesday, Friday and Saturday) spread out throughout the year in Advent, Lent, around Pentecost and in September. And within religious orders – especially enclosed communities – there remains an emphasis on fasting and abstinence. Especially within female orders, this has been linked to anorexia.

'Holy anorexia'

The link between women's sinfulness and food is made at the very start of the Bible, when Eve's desire for the apple brings about the destruction of Paradise. It reached a high point in mediaeval Christianity when many women saints literally fasted themselves to death in what subsequent scholars have labelled 'holy anorexia'. The best-known case is that of Saint Catherine of Siena who would only eat bread, raw herbs and water and starved herself to death. She is sometimes called the first anorexic, but Saint Margaret of Cortona (1247–97) has an earlier claim. She worked ceaselessly amongst the needy of her home city and wrote: 'I want to die of starvation to satiate the poor.' Some of these mediaeval women saints refused all other food than the host at daily Eucharistic services. Saint Veronica Giuliani (1660–1727) was denying herself food when she developed stigmata – the marks of the crucified Christ – on her body. The imprint of the crown of thorns, pressed on to Jesus on his way to Calvary, could reportedly be seen on her. The Carmelite Saint Mary Magdalen de'Pazzi (1566–1607) was another who took up extreme fasting to show her solidarity with the poor.

Eucharistic fasting

Catholics used to be required to fast from midnight on the day before they received the Eucharist as recognition of their spiritual hunger and thirst for Jesus. This was undertaken in imitation of Christ, who fasted for 40 days before beginning his public ministry. In the Beatitudes, set out in the Sermon on the Mount, Jesus said: 'Happy are those who hunger and thirst for what is right: they shall be satisfied' (Mt 5:6).

However, in November 1964 Pope Paul VI reduced this period of fasting to one hour. *The Code of Canon Law* states: 'One who is to receive the Most Holy Eucharist is to abstain from any food or drink, with the exception of water and medicine, for at least the period of one hour before Holy Communion.'

The current rule allows for exceptions. If a priest celebrates more than one Mass on the same day, as often happens on Sunday, he is only bound to the one-hour fast before the first Mass. And those over the age of 60 or ill are exempt, though a 15-minute fast, if possible, is recommended.

These directives are not, however, followed as rigorously as they once were. Pope John Paul II lamented the fact in his apostolic letter, *Dominicae Cenae* ('On the Mystery of the Eucharist') of 1980: 'What one finds most often is not so much a feeling of unworthiness as a certain lack of interior willingness, if one may use this expression, a lack of Eucharistic "hunger" and "thirst", which is also a sign of lack of adequate sensitivity towards the great sacrament of love and a lack of understanding of its nature.'

Conclusion

The practice of individual Catholics may be changing faster than the relaxation by Rome of certain regulations over fasting and abstinence, but at the heart of the sacramental and devotional life of Catholicism remains a bedrock of practice and belief that dates back to the earliest times of the Church. The Mass, the Eucharist, the sacraments are the very heart of what it means to be a Catholic.

11

the sacred and the secular

In this chapter you will learn:
- where Catholic teaching clashes with secular orthodoxy
- how the annulment process works
- why abortion is such a key issue.

All Christian denominations have a view of human sexuality that sits unhappily with many of the attitudes of modern, secular society. However, Catholicism enjoys a particular reputation for taking a conservative stance on a whole range of issues from sex before marriage and homosexuality, through to the appropriate response to the AIDS pandemic. Sometimes criticism of the Church is based on an outdated perception of what it does actually teach. And even when that teaching is accurately conveyed before being attacked, the background to it is often not explained, leaving an impression that Catholicism is restrictive of sexual freedoms as a way of exercising control over Catholics' lives. While there may have been some truth in this assertion in mediaeval times – when Catholicism had ambitions to dominate every aspect of the lives of every person in Europe – in more recent times controversial rulings tend to spring from two sources:

- a concern to direct humankind away from what the Church sees as potentially sinful behaviour that offends against God's law
- a belief that the passing moral codes of any particular era need to be seen in the broader context of human history.

Catholics and sex

Catholics are forbidden to have sex before or outside marriage. This also used to be the attitude of Western society, shaped as it has been by Christian teaching. However, as Christian teaching has become less influential, secular codes of behaviour have changed, and different choices have become generally acceptable, leaving Catholicism seemingly isolated in sticking to traditional notions of right and wrong in this area.

In times past, even in the most Church-dominated societies, there were always those who took no notice of Christian moral strictures about sexual relationships outside marriage. However, back then, governments believed that marriage was the bedrock of a stable society and so tended to join with the Church in legislating on the basis of its teachings on the subject. Today's politicians, by contrast, tend to place the emphasis more on the family, regardless of whether parents are married or living together, straight or gay. Their concerns are essentially practical and pragmatic – how to create viable units as the building blocks of a stable society.

For Catholicism, though, there remains the overarching moral dimension. The primary purpose of sex, it believes, is the procreation of children, and the correct context for creating children is within a marriage. So sex must be restricted to married, heterosexual couples.

Despite the Church's constant restatement of this position, it no longer appears to be one followed even by the majority of Catholics – especially in Western society. Many will have several relationships before finding a life partner, and many will co-habit before marriage without ever feeling the need either to confess this in the sacrament of reconciliation, or to stop going to the Eucharist as a result. The concept of 'living in sin', as it was once called, is no longer relevant to many Catholics. Some go further and resent the emphasis that Catholicism continues to place on what it regards as sexual sin in contrast to other transgressions – economic and fiscal crimes, for instance – that will potentially impact on the lives of many more people.

Catholicism would answer that this emphasis on sex is found in equal measure in secular society. As the Vatican's 1975 *Declaration on Sexual Ethics* put it: 'In the present period, the corruption of morals has increased, and one of the most serious indications of this corruption is the unbridled exaltation of sex.'

Catholicism was not the first religion to regard sexual licence as dangerous. The Greek philosopher Plato (424–348 BC), for instance, taught that the human body was evil because it distracted the mind from the pursuit of truth. He saw sex as a function of the body. Aristotle (384–322 BC), his pupil, shared this view and regarded women as inferior to men and too ready to distract them with sex from cerebral matters. Both Aristotle and Plato were crucial in shaping Catholic thinking, most notably through Saint Thomas Aquinas who used their writings as the basis of his own highly influential teachings in the thirteenth century.

The resulting impression that Catholics have to choose between a life of spiritual fulfilment or sexual fulfilment was well summed-up by the convent-educated twentieth-century novelist, Antonia White, best remembered for *Frost in May*. 'My chief difficulties,' she wrote in her diaries, 'about the Church centre around her attitude to sex. So a case could evidently be made out for the Church being an alternative to sexual life. Whatever the truth is, it is certainly a fact that, in my own life, I have always had an either/or attitude about sex and the spiritual life.'

The Second Vatican Council did, however, make some inroads into the prevailing essentially negative perception held by Catholicism of sex. In *Gaudium et Spes* (1965), it is stated: 'Married love is uniquely expressed and perfected by the exercise of the acts proper to marriage. Hence the acts in marriage by which the intimate and chaste union of all spouses take place are noble and honourable.'

Contraception

Catholicism, as we have already seen, reasserted its ban on artificial contraception in 1968 in the encyclical *Humanae vitae* on the grounds that the pill, condoms and other devices interfered with the transmission of human life. The 'unitative' part – the pleasure – of sex cannot be separated, it said, from the 'procreative'.

This teaching has not been faithfully observed by many Catholics. The Church does, however, support other forms of 'natural' family planning. It thereby endorses the desire of many Catholic couples to limit the number of children they have – for economic, health and psychological reasons. It is a question of means. In his 1981 encyclical, *Familiaris Consortio* ('On the Christian Family in the Modern World'), John Paul II wrote: 'The choice of the natural rhythms involves accepting the cycle of the person, that is, the woman, and thereby accepting dialogue, reciprocal respect, shared responsibility and self control.'

However, some of the techniques Catholicism recommends – most of which involve identifying the times each month when women are fertile and abstaining from sex during those periods – are complicated and have lower success rates than 'artificial' means. And many would not accept any essential difference in terms of purpose between 'natural' and 'artificial' contraception.

Abortion

Human life begins, the Catholic Church teaches, at the moment the egg is fertilized by the sperm. From that moment forward, what medicine calls an embryo is, in Catholic eyes, an unborn child. Abortion is therefore the destruction of that life and a sin. This is a constant position that stretches back throughout the history of the Church. In *City of God*, Saint Augustine

(354–430) condemned those 'depraved married persons' who use poisons to 'stifle within the womb and eject the foetus that has been conceived… [They] do not deserve the name of husband and wife… it was not for wedlock but for fornication that they became united.'

Catholicism has been prominent in the campaign to prevent the legalization of abortion around the world and, where it already exists, to have it outlawed or access limited. Its efforts, though well supported and well reported, have achieved few successes with legislators, even in devoutly Catholic countries such as Italy and Ireland. While Catholicism does not support the antics of those pro-life activists who direct violence towards abortion clinics and those who work in them, it does (in the Vatican's 1974 *Declaration of Procured Abortion*, for instance) attempt to portray abortion as part of a wider 'contraceptive mentality', where the ready availability of contraceptive pills creates a climate in which, if those pills fail to stop conception, recourse to abortion seems a natural step.

Some Catholic leaders also place the Church's stance on abortion within the context of its broader defence of human life. To be pro-life, the then leader of Catholics in England and Wales, Cardinal Basil Hume (1923–99) stated on numerous occasions, was to demand not only an end to abortion but support for parents, decent homes, schools and hospitals, and job prospects for all. His counterpart in Scotland, Cardinal Thomas Winning (1925–2001), also demanded that Church opposition to abortion be matched by practical steps to offer real support, for example, in the form of supported housing, to those women who were contemplating abortion because they could not face bringing a child into the world alone.

Assisted conception

Catholicism sees having children as one of the prime purposes of marriage and procreation as indivisibly linked with sex. However, it warns Catholic couples against seeing having children as a right, and teaches that they are a gift from God.

It bars couples struggling to have a child naturally from most forms of assisted conception. With over 3 million children in the world now having been born through IVF (*in vitro* fertilization techniques) according to statistics released in 2006, the Church's opposition is another example of it setting its face against secular society. The grounds for its opposition have been set out many times, but are found with great clarity in *Donum vitae* ('The Gift of Life'), a 1987 document from the Vatican's Congregation for the Doctrine of the Faith. It sets out three principal objections to standard means of assisted conception which use *in vitro* fertilization methods:

1 That more than one egg at a time is fertilized outside the wife's body by the husband's sperm, and that 'spare' embryos created by this process may subsequently be destroyed or used in experimentation (e.g. to generate stem-cells for research). This contradicts the Church's teaching on the dignity of human life, since from the moment of conception, the fertilized egg is regarded by Catholicism as a human life.

2 That artificial insemination and IVF separate sex and procreation. 'Contraception deliberately deprives the conjugal act of its openness to procreation... Homologous artificial fertilization, in seeking a procreation which is not the fruit of a specific act of conjugal union, objectively effects an analogous separation between the goods and the meanings of marriage.' So where *Humanae vitae* says you cannot have sex without procreation, *Donum vitae* argues, by association, you cannot have procreation without sex.

3 That artificial insemination normally requires the husband to masturbate and that this is 'another sign of this dissociation' between sex and procreation. 'Even when it is done for the purposes of procreation, the act remains deprived of its unitative meaning. It lacks the sexual relationship called for by the moral order.'

There are forms of IVF that some Catholics believe do not offend against the laws of the Church – like aspects of the GIFT (gametes intra-fallopian transfer) technique which can involve the simple act of transferring an egg from the woman's ovary to the lower end of her fallopian tube to overcome a blockage, after which conception can take place in the natural way.

Homosexuality

Though the New Testament contains condemnations of homosexuality from, amongst others, Saint Paul – 'men doing shameless things with men' (Romans 1:26–27) – it is not a subject that Jesus addresses. Catholicism has, however, long maintained an absolute condemnation of homosexuality, listing it (alongside homicide, depriving workers of their pay, and oppressing widows and orphans) as one of four sins 'crying out to heaven for vengeance'.

In more recent times, though, with modern society discarding old prejudices against gays and lesbians, the Church has also adapted its position. It now condemns all discrimination and persecution of homosexuals. It also makes a distinction between 'orientation' – i.e. being a man who is attracted sexually to other men, or a woman to other women – and giving 'expression' to that orientation – by having a sexual relationship. The second is 'intrinsically disordered', according to the Vatican's 1975 *Declaration on Sexual Ethics*, 'and can in no case be approved of', but the first is permissible, though it remains 'a serious depravity' and 'the sad consequence of rejecting God'.

Many openly gay Catholics, who continue to attend the sacraments, despite living in long-standing partnerships, would reply that they have not rejected God, but are, in fact, as God made them. Civil laws in European countries to permit civil partnerships between gay couples were denounced in 2003 by the Vatican as 'the legislation of evil'.

AIDS

When the AIDS pandemic began to make headlines in the 1980s, the Catholic Church's response was a limited one because it, like many others at the time, saw AIDS as something affecting only gay men. That belief has since been comprehensively disproved. The Church has subsequently stepped up its efforts to offer non-judgemental care and support for the many individuals and families around the world affected by HIV/AIDS.

Catholicism remains opposed, though, to the policies of international medical agencies, governments and the UN to encourage condom use as a way of preventing the transmission of AIDS. Catholicism's message is that abstinence outside marriage and fidelity within are the best ways of avoiding spreading infection.

It has even argued that a condom cannot be described as 'safe' because it may split. Cardinal Alfonso Lopez Trujillo, President of the Vatican's Council for the Family, caused headlines in 2004 when he claimed that condoms, even when they did not split, offered inadequate protection against the transmission of the virus because they were permeable. His suggestions have subsequently been disproved by scientists.

Sexual abuse

In the 1990s, Catholicism faced a growing number of complaints about priests who had abused children in their care over many decades. It was further shown that, even when the identity of some of these paedophile priests had been made known to Church authorities, they had simply been moved to other parishes and allowed to continue their abuse by bishops keen to keep such stories out of the newspapers. When some of the cases reached court – in Ireland, Australia, America, Canada, the United Kingdom and elsewhere – the Catholic Church was ordered to pay substantial damages. Even larger sums have been agreed in out of court settlements and some dioceses – especially in the United States – have faced financial ruin as a result.

In response to the revelations, many local bishops' conferences have now undertaken root and branch reforms of their child protection procedures and introduced new guidelines, working closely with civil authorities to ensure that no such abuse or cover-up of that abuse can take place again. Since Benedict XVI became Pope, he has given new impetus to this process. He has removed the Vatican's protection from some prominent figures accused of abuse and has spoken of his pain at the whole unhappy chapter in Catholicism and the damage caused to innocent lives.

The revelations have done great damage to the reputation of Catholicism and to the trust traditionally placed in its priests, the vast majority of whom have had no part in such abuse. It has also prompted a new focus on vetting procedures in seminaries with a view to picking out potential abusers at an early stage, and on the on-going training and evaluation of priests and deacons so as to spot and act on any warning signs of inappropriate behaviour.

Annulment

The Church's belief that marriage is for life is based on Jesus's words in Matthew's gospel: '... that is why a man must leave father and mother, and cling to his wife, and the two become one body. They are no longer two, therefore, but one body. So then, what God has united, man must not divide.'

Civil divorce is not recognized by Catholicism and, though obtaining a civil divorce does not bar either husband or wife from the sacraments, if either partner subsequently remarries in a civil service, he or she can be. To avoid this scenario, the Church offers the annulment procedure.

Unlike civil divorce, which is based on the differences between the couple that make their marriage unsustainable, annulment seeks evidence that the marriage was null – i.e. invalid – usually from the very start. To obtain an annulment, either partner in a Catholic marriage has to approach their local diocese, via their parish priest, and face a tribunal, which will examine if there are grounds for declaring that marriage null and void.

The annulment tribunal has nothing to do with financial settlements and the custody of children, and concerns itself only with trying to ascertain if a Catholic marriage has ever existed. If it decides there are grounds for allowing an annulment, that decision must be verified by a second tribunal in another diocese in the same country. If the two agree, the parties to the original marriage are now free to marry again in church. Though their marriage is declared null, the Church stresses that any children born of that marriage are not illegitimate.

If the two tribunals disagree, however, the case is referred to the Sacred Rota, Catholicism's central court in Rome, for a final decision. It is called the Rota – from the Latin for wheel – because originally the court sat in the round. While the bulk of its caseload concerns annulments, it also hears appeals on other aspects of canon law.

Grounds for declaring a marriage null include (as set out in the *Code of Canon Law*):

- insufficient or impaired use of reason during the marriage ceremony by either partner
- grave lack of judgement in making the decision to marry, including a misunderstanding of what marriage is about, or immature consent to it
- fraud – that one partner was intentionally deceived about the presence or absence of a quality in the other
- wilful exclusion of children – that one partner, either explicitly or implicitly, intended to refuse to have sex with a view to conceiving a child

- wilful exclusion of marital fidelity – that one partner married intending, either explicitly or implicitly, not to remain faithful
- impotence – that one partner was unable to have sex.

Conclusion

The Catholic Church's teachings about various aspects of sex, relationships and conception remain controversial and out of step with many of the beliefs of the rest of society. Many Catholics do not follow to the letter the Vatican's rulings on such matters. For those who do, there can be much pain in the seeming gap between the realities of their lives and the ideals of the Church. However, there is a clear logic to the Church's insistence that human life begins at the moment of conception and is an inviolable gift from God that links many of the teachings in this area.

12

dissent and dispute

In this chapter you will learn:
- about the role of conscience in Catholicism
- about Church suspicion of mystics
- how liberation theology developed.

The paramount role in a Catholic's life of a well-informed conscience has been a key part of the Church's moral teaching for centuries. Personal conscience, according to Saint Thomas Aquinas in the thirteenth century, should be the ultimate guide in all moral questions. It was, he said, the medium through which a human being received God's directives. He placed the dictate of conscience above any rules laid out by a human authority – including ecclesiastical ones.

There was an echo of Aquinas in the oft-quoted words of Cardinal John Henry Newman (1801–90) in his 1875 letter to the Duke of Norfolk: 'If I am obliged to bring religion into after-dinner toasts (which indeed does not seem quite the thing) I shall drink – to the Pope, if you please – still, to Conscience first, and to the Pope afterwards.'

The Second Vatican Council, in its declaration on religious liberty, *Dignitatis Humanae* (1965), upheld the primacy of conscience. 'In all his activity, a man is bound to follow his conscience in order that he may come to God, the end and purpose of life. It follows that he is not to be forced to act in a manner contrary to his conscience. Nor, on the other hand, is he to be restrained from acting in accordance with his conscience, especially in matters religious.'

However, the Council made an important distinction in this regard between infallible and non-infallible teachings. 'A Catholic who feels compelled to dissent ... from infallible teaching ... has no option but to sever his connection with the Church. On the other hand, when the question at issue is the obligatory force of non-definitive teaching ... then Catholics may dissent from such teaching for serious conscientious reasons and still consider themselves to be in full communion with the Church.'

The question of conscience and the role of loyal dissent remains a delicate one in modern Catholicism. Pope John Paul II, in his message for World Peace Day in 1999, stressed once again the primacy of conscience: 'People are obliged to follow their conscience in all circumstances and cannot be forced to act against it.' Yet, there were those who felt that sometimes such words were directed more at the situation of religious believers who live in lands where the government wishes to clamp down on their freedom to worship. When it comes to dissent within the Church, Catholicism does place practical limits on freedom of conscience.

The Internal Forum

There was a lively debate in Catholicism during the papacy of Pope John Paul II about the wide application of what is called in Canon Law 'The Internal Forum'. This concept falls short of the Protestant idea that each individual believer must right his conscience via his personal relationship with God. Catholicism still insists on an intermediary role for the priest, between believer and God. But in this wider interpretation of the Internal Forum, a priest in the sacrament of Reconciliation would not require a Catholic whose life fell short of the Church's ideals – someone living in a stable gay relationship, for instance, or who had remarried outside the Church without seeking an annulment – to promise to change those life circumstances before he or she received absolution. The Internal Forum was seen as a way of avoiding large numbers of otherwise faithful Catholics feeling they were excluded from the Eucharist.

The concept was based on canon 130 of the 1983 *Code of Canon Law*: 'Of itself, the power of governance is exercised by the External Forum; sometimes, however, it is exercised by the Internal Forum only, but in such a way that the effects which its exercise is designed to have in the External Forum are not acknowledged in that forum, except in so far as the law prescribes this for determinate cases.' Essentially, this approach allows Catholics whose lives are publicly regarded as sinful by the Church – i.e. in the External Forum – to reach a private accommodation with their own consciences and their priest – in the Internal Forum.

Many priests regarded it as an overly legal formula for routine pastoral sensitivity. However, Pope Benedict XVI, when he was still Cardinal Joseph Ratzinger, dismissed such a legal formula in 1991, saying that making exceptions for individuals in difficult situations might lead the faithful collectively 'into error and confusion regarding the Church's teaching'. He referred to 'numerous abuses committed under the rubric of the Internal Forum solution'. Yet with the Church's adherence to 'the seal of the confessional', it is impossible for the authorities to police any priest's decision to grant absolution during the sacrament of Reconciliation.

Dissent

Some Catholic historians and theologians would argue that their Church has developed, grown and sustained itself for 2000 years only because it has encountered dissent from within its ranks. Those voices that have questioned Church teaching have been the ones that have often pointed a way forward in the development of doctrine, though in their lifetimes they have often been silenced or ignored voices. One example often quoted is Cardinal Newman, the English Anglican who converted to Catholicism in the middle years of the nineteenth century amid a great storm of interest. In his lifetime, Newman often found his ideas treated with suspicion by his new Church, but in the century after his death he was considered as one of the inspirations of the Second Vatican Council.

Another group which has sometimes been regarded as prophets without honour in their own Church, at least in their lifetimes, has been Catholic mystics. The Church has been cautious about accepting reports of individuals having mystical visions of God, whether they be mediaeval nuns or nineteenth-century peasant girls who say they have seen the Virgin Mary.

Five Catholic mystics

Saint Bernard of Clairvaux (1098–1153) is perhaps best remembered today as a reformer of the monastic movement who inspired the Cistercian order, but his personal asceticism, his total disregard for any of the trappings and comforts of life, as well as his conviction that he was speaking God's truth, even when powerful figures in the Church did not want to hear it, made him many enemies. One cardinal dismissed him as 'that noisy and troublesome frog'. However, his mystical writings remain popular to this day.

Mechthild of Magdeburg (1207–82) was a German nun who recorded, in exuberant and emotional language, her visions of God in *The Flowing Light of The Godhead*. Her claim to theological insight and the criticisms she made as a result of it against Church leaders made her a controversial figure in her lifetime and she was forced in her final years to take refuge in a Cistercian nunnery at Helfta. Despite the enduring popularity of her mystical writings, the Church has refused all appeals to canonize her.

Thomas a Kempis (1380–1471) was a German-born monk, linked with a school of Rhineland mystics. He was a respected scholar in his lifetime, producing many admired commentaries on the Bible. His most enduring work, though, was *Imitation of Christ*, a meditation on the life and blessings of Jesus Christ. Many have pressed for his canonization, but his corpse was reputedly exhumed after his death, and splinters found behind his fingernails. It is said he was therefore buried alive and tried to escape the after life, not appropriate behaviour, according to the Church, for a saint.

Saint John of the Cross (1542–91) was a Spanish Carmelite, poet and mystic, renowned for his co-operation with Teresa of Avila in reforming their religious order, and for his mystical writings. His *Spiritual Canticle* – where the soul is the bride and Jesus the bridegroom – was written in 1578 when he was in prison and being flogged in public every week by opponents of his reforms. His *Dark Night of the Soul*, an account of the journey of a soul from body to union with God, is a classic of mystical literature.

Saint Pio of Pietrelcina (1887–1968), an Italian mystic, better known as Padre Pio, was a controversial figure in his lifetime on account of his claims of experiencing heavenly visions and ecstasies, the miraculous cures reportedly made through his intervention, and the stigmata he bore on his body – the marks of Christ's crucifixion. Senior Vatican officials dismissed him in the 1930s as insane, immoral and as using acid to produce his distinctive markings, but by the time of his death he was treated with respect by the Church and canonized by John Paul II in 2002.

Excommunication

Catholicism has, in the past, employed excommunication – literally exclusion from communion – as a weapon against those within its ranks who challenge papal or episcopal authority. Its use had become so commonplace by the time of the Reformation that the Council of Trent (1545–63) insisted on a slow-down. It ruled:

> Although the sword of excommunication is the very sinews of ecclesiastical discipline and very salutary for keeping the people to the observance of their duty, yet it is to be used with sobriety and great circumspection; seeing that experience teaches that if it be wielded rashly or for slight causes, it is more despised than feared, and works more evil than good. Wherefore, such excommunications which are wont to be issued for the

purpose of provoking a revelation, or on account of things lost or stolen, shall be issued by no one whomsoever but the bishop; and not then, except on account of some uncommon circumstance which moves the bishop thereunto, and after the matter has been by him diligently and very maturely weighed.

Since then, this has largely been the practice of Catholicism. Until recently a distinction was made between major and minor excommunication – the latter a bar placed on individuals from attending the sacraments as a way of encouraging them to repent. However, this has now been abandoned. Such excommunications as there are – and they are extremely few – tend to be of public figures, like the opponent of the Second Vatican Council, Archbishop Marcel Lefebvre, rather than private individuals.

Excommunication, based on an ancient Jewish tradition of banning miscreants from the synagogue, is intended by Catholicism to have a healing power. Since you have to be baptized to be excommunicated, it might be seen as a means of bringing individuals up short and forcing them to reconsider the actions that had brought them into dispute with the Church. Equally, since the sacrament of baptism can never be undone, the door always remains open for the excommunicated to return to the fold.

The power to excommunicate belongs to popes, cardinals and bishops, but the *Code of Canon Law* also sets out the grounds for *latae sententiae*, or automatic, excommunication. By certain actions, Catholics can incur excommunication, even if it is never pronounced by a pope, cardinal or bishop. The onus is placed on the individual to confess their sins, repent and seek absolution. Among 'sins' that incur *latae sententiae* excommunication are:

- apostasy (canon 1364)
- heresy (canon 1364)
- schism (canon 1364)
- desecration of the Eucharist (canon 1367)
- physical violence against the Pope (canon 1370)
- ordination of a bishop without papal approval (canon 1382)
- procurement of a completed abortion (canon 1398).

Liberation theology

High on any list of movements of dissent within modern Catholicism would be the theology of liberation which grew as both an academic and a popular, practical expression of Catholicism in Latin America and Asia in the years after the Second Vatican Council. Its 'preferential option for the poor', endorsed at meetings of Latin American bishops in, first, Medellin in 1968 and then Puebla in 1979, was regarded with suspicion by Pope John Paul II and the then Cardinal Joseph Ratzinger, later Pope Benedict XVI. They repeatedly condemned what they saw as Marxist influence in liberation theology and imposed periods of silence on some of its best-known proponents.

One of those was the Brazilian friar, Leonardo Boff. With his priest brother, Clodovis, he wrote the following question and answer sequence:

Q: How are we to be Christians in a world of destitution and injustice?

A: There can be only one answer: we can be followers of Jesus and true Christians only by making common cause with the poor and working out the gospel of liberation.

Liberation theology, which continues to thrive in Latin America and some areas of Asian Catholicism to this day, despite Vatican hostility, takes the example of Jesus's demand for social justice and uses it to insist on an improvement in the lives of the poor. In pursuit of that, some priests became involved in politics and trade unions – most notably the four clerics who were members of Nicaragua's Sandinista government in the 1980s who were rebuked in public by the Pope for their actions.

John Paul's attitude was, however, ambiguous. He was at one with the liberation theologians in demanding a more equal distribution of the world's goods between rich and poor. At Puebla, though, he warned, 'This conception of Christ as a political figure, a revolutionary, as the subversive of Nazareth, does not tally with the Church's catechism.' In 1984 and 1986 the Church issued major documents on liberation theology. They echoed John Paul's view that the Church should work for the liberation of the poor, but do so in an appropriate way for a Church, inspired not by a political vision of a perfect world, but by helping each human being to find their freedom by redemption from sin.

Four Leading Liberation Theologians

Father Gustavo Gutierrez (b.1928): a Peruvian theologian and Dominican priest who has spent his adult life working with the poor of Lima, Gutierrez is regarded as the founding father of liberation theology. His book, *A Theology of Liberation: History, Politics, Salvation* was published in 1971 and is the standard textbook of liberation theology.

Father Leonardo Boff (b.1938): a Brazilian theologian, philosopher and writer, he was summoned to Rome in 1985 and ordered to endure a year's silence after the Vatican objected to his book *Church: Charism and Power*. In 1992, he was facing another period of silence because Rome wished to avoid his involvement in the 'Earth Summit' in Rio de Janeiro where he teaches, but he decided to leave the priesthood.

Father Tissa Balasuriya (b.1924): a Sri Lankan priest closely associated with the spread of liberation theology in Asia. In 1997, he was excommunicated by the Vatican on account of his writings, but the following year it was rescinded.

Archbishop Helder Camara (1909–99): a forerunner of the liberation theologians and an outspoken opponent of Brazil's authoritarian governments, he is best remembered for his remark: 'When I give food to the poor, they call me a saint. When I ask why they have no food, they call me a communist.' On his retirement, the Vatican replaced him in his archdiocese of Olinda and Recife with a conservative cleric who undid much of the Church social justice network that had been established there.

The Devil

Christianity was not the first religion to believe in an evil spirit, or devil, as a counter-force to God in the world. The origins of the idea of a cosmic battle between good and evil can be traced back through Judaism to Zoroastrianism in ancient Persia in the sixth century BC. However, it was Christianity, and Catholicism in particular, that took the idea of an evil spirit, a face to put to the otherwise intangible reality of evil, and made the figure of the Devil a haunting one in the mind of believers.

In the New Testament, it is the Devil who tries to tempt Jesus away from his divinely-ordained mission, and in life, Catholicism taught, particularly in the mediaeval period, it is the Devil who waits at every turn to woo the faithful away from the path of righteousness into sin and ultimately damnation in hell. In mediaeval churches, the most prominent image was often that of the harrowing of hell, souls caught up in flames and eternal torment.

The last major Church document to deal at length with the Devil came at the Fourth Lateran Council in 1215. In more recent times, Catholicism has spoken rarely on the subject. The *Catechism of the Catholic Church*, published in 1993, makes no more than cursory mentions of the Devil as the 'seductive voice' which lures Adam and Eve in the Garden of Eden, and more generally as a dangerous but ultimately insignificant force compared to God. Catholicism teaches that come Judgement Day there is only final defeat for the Devil to look forward to. His fate is already sealed, according to the Book of Revelation, the final chapter in the Bible. Until that Judgement Day, when Christ will return to earth in triumph, the Devil is left snapping at humanity's heels. 'He can impede but not stop the building of God's kingdom.'

Catholicism has, in its few recent pronouncements on the Devil, moved away from the notion of the Devil as a personality and towards the concept of him as a symbol of evil. 'What are the greatest needs of the Church today?' Pope Paul VI asked rhetorically in November 1972. 'Do not let our answer surprise you as being over-simple or even superstitious and unreal: one of the greatest needs is defence from that evil which is called the Devil.'

Exorcism

The downgrading of the Devil in Catholicism from the role he was given by the mediaeval Church has not been accompanied, however, by a parallel sidelining of the practice of exorcism. The Vatican maintains a network of priest exorcists around the globe and continues to believe that, in rare cases, humans can suffer demonic possession.

In March 1982, Pope John Paul II was reported by the then Prefect of his household, Cardinal Jacques Martin, to have exorcized a young woman himself. Yet even senior exorcists, like Father Gabriel Amorth, who served under both John Paul and Benedict in the diocese of Rome, stress that in the vast majority of cases of those seeking exorcism their problems can be dealt with more effectively by counselling.

The rites of exorcism used by the Catholic Church are based on Jesus's actions in casting out demons from possessed individuals in the gospels (Matthew 12:22–28). There are minor rites of exorcism in the wording of the baptismal service, for instance, or when a priest blesses a new home. The main rite of exorcism remains largely unchanged from that set out in 1614. In 1998, it was subject to minor revisions by the Vatican document *De Exorcismis et Supplicationibus Quibusdom* ('Of Exorcisms and Certain Supplications'). This set out a form of words to be used in Latin, but gave permission for local bishops' conferences to approve translations in local languages. It also approved for continuing use the traditional English prayer of exorcism:

> I command you, unclean spirit, whoever you are, along with all your minions now attacking this servant of God, by the mysteries of the incarnation, passion, resurrection and ascension of our Lord Jesus Christ, by the descent of the Holy Spirit, by the coming of our Lord for judgement, that you tell me by some sign your name, and the day and hour of your departure. I command you, moreover, to obey me to the letter, I who am a minister of God despite my unworthiness; nor shall you be emboldened to harm in any way this creature of God, or the bystanders, or any of their possessions. Depart, then, transgressor. Depart, seducer, full of lies and cunning, foe of virtue, persecutor of the innocent. Give place, abominable creature, give way, you monster, give way to Christ, in whom you found none of your works. For he has already stripped you of your powers and laid waste your kingdom, bound you prisoner and plundered your weapons. He has cast you forth into the outer darkness, where everlasting ruin awaits you and your abettors. You are guilty before his Son, our Lord Jesus Christ, whom you presumed to tempt, whom you dared to nail to the cross. You are guilty before the whole human race, to whom you proffered by your enticements the poisoned cup of death.

The rite of exorcism can only be performed by a priest after he has sought the permission of his bishop. It can include – as well as prayers – the laying on of hands, making the sign of the cross and sprinkling with holy water.

Conclusion

Though Catholicism presents itself as an unchanging creed, it has over the centuries emphasized different aspects of its teachings. Its attitude to the Devil is a good example of how what was once a central feature of Catholic life has been downplayed in later centuries. Equally what was once regarded as a dangerous, or even heretical, theological or practical approach can, again over time, become part of the mainstream. Change, development and refocusing is part of being a living Church.

13

saints and martyrs

In this chapter you will learn:
- how Catholicism makes saints
- about the role of miracles
- why martyrs are not always saints.

The Catholic Church has long realized the value of role models in guiding believers towards good and moral lives. Throughout its history it has created saints to whom Catholics can turn in prayer for inspiration, strength, and succour in times of trouble. Some saints are associated with particular needs – Saint Jude, for example, is traditionally associated with hopeless causes. In recent times, however, Pope John Paul II accelerated significantly the saint-making process and created during his 27-year pontificate more saints than had emerged in Catholicism during the past 500 years under his predecessors.

Canonization and beatification

Before 1234, the process of saint making was carried out in Catholicism by popular acclaim. Individuals would be so esteemed after their death that their lives, or legends, would persist within the Church. This was particularly true of those who were martyred for their faith in the early years of Christianity. Stephen, a Jewish convert and deacon, is reported by the Acts of the Apostles (Chapters 6 and 7) to have been stoned to death because of his missionary work. He is regarded by Catholicism as the first martyr and the first saint. His powers as a preacher and miracle worker might be seen as setting the template for all subsequent saints.

However, this democratic system could be erratic. Often stories of different individuals would end up conflated. There is, for example, a clutch of early women saints (Pelagia, Apollinaris, Euphrosyne, Eugenia and Marina) who dressed as men to achieve ascetic lives and whose stories bear a remarkable similarity. And some early saints – Christopher, beloved of drivers, or Valentine, patron of lovers – are now thought never to have existed at all. Their biographies were based on earlier pagan gods, subsumed into the early Christian Church.

One of the earliest Catholic beliefs was in the 'communion of saints', reborn in heaven, marked out by their haloes (rings of light around their heads in traditional depictions) and acting as intermediaries between humanity and God. Hence individuals would chose a saint's name in baptism and later chose a saint as their guardian in confirmation. There would be novenas – or sets of prayers to be recited regularly – to individual saints. The cult of the martyred dead became part of Christianity's promise of eternal life.

Haloes

The use of haloes in religious art predates Christianity. A ring of light above the head to mark out gods is seen in Ancient Egyptian and Asian depictions, as well as in regard to Greek and Roman gods. Christianity first took up the practice around the fourth century, originally only for pictures of Jesus, but quickly the practice spread. There is a hierarchy of haloes in Christian art. Triangular ones are reserved for the three persons of the Trinity – Father, Son and Holy Spirit. Round haloes, in white, gold or yellow, are for saints. The Virgin Mary has a circle of stars. A square halo would be used when depicting a living but saintly figure as, for example, in paintings of various popes. And Judas is traditionally given a black halo. Some artists would give Mary a mandorla, or all-body halo. The practice of depicting saints with haloes began to die out in the Renaissance period.

Central control of saint making

As the leaders of the Church grew in their ambitions to regulate and orchestrate the lives of the faithful, the process of creating popular saints was also taken under control. In 1234, Pope Gregory IX published his *Decretals* – or collection of laws – in which he claimed for the Bishop of Rome absolute power over the causes of saints. Since they were objects of devotion throughout the Church, he argued, only the Pope, with universal jurisdiction, could possess the authority to canonize (or make into a saint).

It is from this point onwards that the system, still largely in operation in the Vatican today, began to operate. The range of candidates elevated to sainthood became narrower and greater proof, both of their virtues in life and of their intervention from beyond the grave, was demanded.

Integral to the Catholic process of saint making is the necessity for miracles. To become a saint, an individual, once dead, must be shown, to the satisfaction of the Church authorities (today the Congregation for the Causes of Saints), to have answered the prayers of the faithful for his or her intercession with God. The most straightforward 'proof' of this is that those praying to the would-be saint have then been miraculously cured. In the present system, proof of one miracle (the congregation employs doctors on its evaluation panel) is required for the candidate to be beatified – declared Blessed – and two for them to be canonized – named a Saint.

Between 1234 and 1978, there had been fewer than 300 successful candidates for the sainthood. The Church's habit was to ponder long and hard on its decisions, often taking more than 100 years to reach a verdict, and to promote only those of exceptional virtue.

John Paul II took a different approach. In one year alone (1988) he canonized 122 men and women. In total, he made 476 saints and approved 1315 beatifications. The canonization or beatification ceremony of a local figure became a central part of his many trips around the world.

Inevitably, it meant that the length of time spent scrutinizing cases was shorter and saints would be named soon after their deaths. The two most notable examples of this were Mother Teresa of Calcutta, who was beatified within six years of her death in 1997, and Monsignor Josemaria Escriva, founder of the Opus Dei movement, canonized in 2002, 27 years after his death.

Escriva's beatification (in 1992) and canonization were particularly controversial with critics – including a former leader of Spain's Catholic Church who argued that it was 'a scandal'. It was pointed out that, particularly with a figure whose legacy was disputed (Opus Dei is not a universally admired organization within Catholicism), the more traditional route of waiting many years before making a final decision would be more appropriate. Question marks too were raised over the cost of the whole canonization process. Opus Dei had dedicated significant resources towards ensuring the rapid progress of the Escriva cause through the Vatican's systems. Other causes did not have such backing and hence would take longer.

However, the speed with which it was processed gives a clue to John Paul II's own motivations in making so many saints. He was keen to hold up to Catholics, and to the world, figures whom he believed embodied in their lives and achievements the essential Catholic values. Opus Dei, for instance, was a favourite organization of his in its fight against the expansion of secular values. He had given it the status of a personal prelature – answering only to him and not to the local bishop in diocese where it operated.

Ten patron saints

1 **Alcoholics**: Saint Monica (322–87), mother of Saint Augustine, who was forced to endure a brutal marriage in the house of her unfriendly in-laws.

2 **Choirboys**: Saint Dominic Savio (1842–57), one of the youngest saints, a model student in his native Italy and an early co-worker of Saint John Bosco in founding the Salesian order, but died of lung disease.

3 **Foundry workers**: Saint Agatha (d.251), Early Church virgin-martyr from southern Italy, credited with stopping an eruption of the volcano, Mount Etna.

4 **Hairdressers**: Saint Martin de Porres (1579–1639), lived and worked with the poor in his native Peru, calling himself a 'poor slave', but in his youth had been apprenticed to a barber.

5 **Internet**: Saint Isidore of Seville (560–636), learned Spaniard who produced many books and an enduring encyclopedia.

6 **Lawyers**: Saint Thomas More (1478–1535), English lawyer who, though Henry VIII's chancellor, refused to sign his Oath of Supremacy out of loyalty to the Pope and was executed.

7 **Musicians**: Saint Cecilia (third century), high-born Christian convert and martyr, who reputedly survived three attempts to cut off her head and bequeathed her Roman house as a church. She is usually portrayed with a viola or at a small organ.

8 **Orphans**: Saint Jerome Emiliani (1481–1537), Venetian soldier who embraced Catholicism while in prison and set up three orphanages on his release.

9 **Rheumatism**: Saint James the Greater, one of the original 12 Apostles called by Jesus.

10 **Undertakers**: Saint Joseph of Arimathea, who offered his tomb to the Apostles as a place to bury Jesus after his crucifixion.

Modern martyrs

The connection between martyrdom and sainthood was a feature of the early Church, and in more recent times the example of a number of figures who have died for their faith has continued to inspire Catholics, even if their causes for canonization have not always merited fast-tracking by the Vatican.

Archbishop Oscar Romero (1917–80): Archbishop of San Salvador for the last three years of his life, an outspoken opponent of the rulers of his country, and 'the voice of the voiceless' who spoke up for the mass of peasants who today already regard him as a saint. He was gunned down by soldiers at the altar as he said Mass in March 1980. The process for his beatification has begun but is moving slowly

Bishop Juan Gerardi (1922–98): Survived one assassination attempt in 1980, but was killed soon after completing a report on human rights' abuses in his native Guatemala. His murder was condemned by Pope John Paul II. Two soldiers were later convicted of the crime.

Father Jerzy Popieluszko (1947–84): Charismatic priest, close to the trade union Solidarity, and part of the struggle to free Poland of its Soviet-backed communist government. After repeated harassment, his body was found in a reservoir in October 1984. About 250,000 Poles attended his funeral.

Father Maximilian Kolbe (1894–1941): Franciscan priest who died at the hands of the Nazis in the Auschwitz Concentration Camp when he volunteered to take the place of another in the gas chambers. He was canonized in 1982 and described as a 'martyr for charity' and, by John Paul II, 'the patron of our difficult century'.

The seven monk-martyrs of Tibhirine: In March 1996, Islamic fundamentalists, involved in a brutal conflict with the Algerian government, abducted seven French Cistercian monks from the monastery of Our Lady of Atlas, near Tibhirine. Seven weeks later they killed them.

Conclusion

The Vatican has now slowed the speed of canonizations once more, but the example of saints and martyrs remains central to Catholics' lives. The inspiration offered by figures from throughout the two millennia of the Church's history remains a distinctive part of Catholicism's liturgies, prayers, literature and art.

14

where two worlds overlap

In this chapter you will learn:
- about the relationship of religion and science
- who are Catholic writers
- why Opus Dei is so controversial.

The Second Vatican Council was all about encouraging a new relationship between Catholicism and the modern world, casting away old hostilities and the Church taking its place once more as a full participant in global affairs. This is largely what has followed, but such a level of engagement brings with it renewed scrutiny and fresh challenges.

In the political arena, the Church has found itself called on to make moral pronouncements on global conflicts and the arms' race. The neutral position of Pius XII in World War II or Benedict XV in the Great War has been replaced by outspoken advocacy on the part of John Paul II, in particular of the fight for freedom from Soviet overlordship in eastern Europe. Age-old Catholic teaching about what constitutes a just war and how far each nation has the right to defend itself has been redefined in the light of contemporary contexts.

And in the broader social, cultural and scientific spheres of the modern world, Catholicism has found itself involved, discussed and criticized but, more crucially, also called upon to think afresh about traditional positions and new challenges.

Religion and science

The relationship between religion and science has long been a fraught one. Catholicism, in particular, has often resented and repressed the claims of scientists, though in more recent times a more productive dialogue has emerged, spearheaded by the Vatican's own Academy of Science.

Athanasius Kircher

In the seventeenth century, the Jesuit, Father Athanasius Kircher, was widely celebrated across Europe for his books that combined scientific and spiritual discovery. 'Painter and poet say in vain, he's here,' reads the Latin inscription beneath the portrait that graced his books, 'his face and name are known throughout earth's sphere.' With the approval of his religious superiors and of the many senior clerics who were his friends, Kircher covered a dizzying range of subjects – geology, mathematics and magnetism. He invented, among other devices, a water-powered organ. In 1678 he opened the world's first public museum with displays on science, and corresponded with Galileo, Newton and Descartes. Science, he believed, was the way to penetrate the workings of the Divine Mind. The human, the divine and the scientific came together as one.

Until the mediaeval period, Catholic thinkers believed that science should be a subsidiary branch of religion and worked to synthesize its discoveries with the teachings of the Church. That endeavour, however, became progressively more difficult and raised the issue that still stands at the heart of the dispute between religion and science – namely that they use very different methodologies. Catholicism is concerned with faith; science with proof. Most Catholics would say that they could not, empirically, prove the existence of God or Jesus's resurrection, but they believe in them. Most scientists would reply that their faith therefore is not soundly based.

A measure of how and when the relationship between Catholicism and science first became fraught can be seen in the treatment of the Tuscan physicist, mathematician and astronomer, Galileo Galilei (1564–1642), today often called 'the father of modern science'. Galileo was a friend of popes and a Catholic, but attracted controversy because he spoke out publicly with the view that the earth revolved around a stationary sun. Catholicism, taking its lead from the Old Testament, officially rejected this position, though many senior figures accepted that Galileo was right. In 1633, he was summoned before the Inquisition, forced to recant his views, and placed under house arrest for the remainder of his life. His writings were banned, until 1718, and remained on the Church's *Index of Forbidden Books* until 1835. However, in 1992, Pope John Paul II, in the course of encouraging a new working relationship between religion and science, made a public statement of regret for the way in which the Church had treated Galileo.

As the Scientific Enlightenment, initiated by outstanding individuals like Galileo, gathered pace in the eighteenth century, Catholicism retreated ever more from any contact with science and was distrustful of its practitioners. When in 1859, Charles Darwin published his *Origin of the Species*, Catholicism could only condemn outright the idea that humanity was the product of an evolutionary process.

However, in 1950 in *Humani Generis*, Pope Pius XII endorsed the first flickering of a rapprochement. He wrote that he did not forbid debate between Catholics and the scientific community on evolution and other associated matters. Others, like the French Jesuit and palaeontologist, Father Pierre Teilhard de Chardin (1881–1955), were already working on a theology in books like *The Phenomenon of Man* that would bring together the theory of evolution with the account of the world's creation by God in the Book of Genesis. It is as a result of such work that Catholicism has refused to countenance such theories supported by evangelical Christians as creationism – that the world was literally made in seven days by God – or intelligent design (that God created matter and then worked through natural evolution).

In 1996, Pope John Paul II all but gave Darwin his approval when he described evolution as 'no longer a mere hypothesis'. He went on: 'It is indeed remarkable that this theory [evolution] has been progressively accepted by researchers, following a series of discoveries in various fields of knowledge. The convergence, neither sought nor fabricated, of the results of the work that was conducted independently is in itself a significant argument in favour of this theory.'

Today the exchange between Catholicism and science takes place at many levels:

- In co-operation between clerics and psychiatrists and psychologists over those presenting themselves with what they describe as signs of demonic possession.
- Over research into infertility where the Church opposes scientific work that creates 'spare embryos' (in Catholic eyes, human lives) for the purpose of research.
- In the Church urging scientists who wish to use stem cells in research, to investigate the well-attested alternative sources of such cells other than embryos.
- In the Church's own processes for scrutinizing claims of miraculous cures, made as a result of visits to shrines or in support of appeals to canonize individuals. The Church is assisted by a panel of scientists in examining such claims and seeking out any scientific explanation of what has occurred.

Pius XI set up the Pontifical Academy of Science in 1936, in its current form, with the aim of promoting 'progress of the mathematical, physical and natural sciences, and the study of related epistemological questions and issues'. It works in six fields:

- fundamental science
- the science and technology of global questions and issues
- science designed to assist the developing world
- the ethics and politics of science
- bioethics
- epistemology (the theory of knowledge).

Around a third of its members at any time are Nobel laureates.

The 'just war'

In recent years, religion has often been held to lie at the base of all the conflicts in the world. No distinction is made, in making such charges, between good religion, faithful to the teachings and traditions of that faith, and bad religion, erroneous or partial interpretations of its beliefs to suit a particular purpose.

In the New Testament, Jesus gives differing messages about whether it can ever be right to resort to violence to solve conflicts. In Matthew's Gospel (5:39), he warns: 'I say this to you: offer the wicked man no resistance. On the contrary, if anyone hits you on the right cheek, offer the other as well.' But this pacifist impulse is checked later (Luke 22:36) when he tells his followers: 'But now, if you have a purse take it; if you have a haversack, do the same; if you have no sword, sell your cloak and buy one.'

Saint Augustine was the first Catholic thinker to try to steer a course between these apparently opposite imperatives. He was reacting in the fourth century to the invasion of Rome and the need to defend the city against the Barbarians. In *The City of God*, he set out the 'just war' theory. It has remained at the heart of Catholicism ever since. The conditions for a just war are set out in the *Catechism*. It writes:

> The strict conditions for legitimate defence by military force require rigorous consideration. The gravity of such a decision makes it subject to rigorous conditions of moral legitimacy. At one and the same time:
>
> - the damage inflicted by the aggressor on the nation or community of nations must be lasting, grave, and certain
> - all other means of putting an end to it must have been shown to be impractical or ineffective
> - there must be serious prospects of success
> - the use of arms must not produce evils and disorders graver than the evil to be eliminated. The power of modern means of destruction weighs very heavily in evaluating this condition.
>
> These are the traditional elements enumerated in what is called the 'just war' doctrine. The evaluation of these conditions for moral legitimacy belongs to the prudential judgement of those who have responsibility for the common good.

These are hard criteria to meet, and the presumption in modern Catholicism is against war. Particularly with the sophistication and power of modern weaponry, and the advent of nuclear arsenals with huge destructive power, some theologians would argue that it is now impossible for the criteria for a just war ever to be met. Pope Paul VI appeared to share their view when in 1965, in his historic address to the United Nations, he appealed: 'war no more, war never again!' And, as if to emphasize the same point, Pope John Paul II condemned the first Gulf War in 1991 on no less than 56 separate occasions, while he described the 2003 invasion of Iraq as 'a defeat for humanity' with no justification morally and legally. As America and its allies toppled Saddam Hussein, John Paul reiterated his view that 'violence and arms can never resolve the problems of the world'.

On the wider question of the moral legitimacy of nuclear weapons, the Catholic Church has expressed its profound misgivings, but the Vatican has never condemned the policy of nuclear deterrence outright. Individual bishops' conferences around the world have, however, taken a more forthright stance, while individual Catholic clerics – like Monsignor Bruce Kent in Britain in the 1980s as leader of the Campaign for Nuclear Disarmament – have demanded the scrapping of nuclear arsenals.

Catholicism and the arts

The Catholic Church has been one of the most significant patrons of the arts over the centuries and remains to this day custodian of some of the most outstanding buildings, paintings, frescoes and sculptures the world has ever seen. However, both the means by which some of these works of art were originally funded – the Basilica of Saint Peter in Rome was paid for, in part, by the sale of indulgences, an abuse that was amongst the complaints of the Protestant reformers – and their on-going custodianship remains controversial.

In modern times, as the Church has placed great emphasis on combating poverty and social justice, the suggestion is often heard that it should dispose of the great works of art it possesses to fund programmes to help the poor. Some bishops have tried to answer these pleas by, for example, selling their ornate palaces and moving into humbler homes amongst the poor of their dioceses. And the Vatican has attempted to turn its great repository for priceless treasures – the Vatican Museum – into a business whose profits go to support the work of the Church. This has only been partially successful. The operation of the Vatican and curia still depends heavily on 'Peter's Pence', the annual offerings of Catholics around the world, made on the Feast of Saint Peter and Saint Paul (June 29).

While the days when Pope Julius II (Pope 1503–13) could commission the greatest artists of the Renaissance – Bramante, Raphael and Michelangelo – to redesign and decorate the Vatican have long since gone, Catholicism remains a noted patron of architects, makers of stained glass and fabric designers who assist it – among others – in restoring, building and decorating churches and designing the vestments used in the liturgy. In the Vatican's collection are, for instance, priests' vestments by the French artist, Henri Matisse (1869–1954).

Among the most notable of modern Catholic churches and cathedrals are:

Barcelona: La Sagrada Familia (in Catalan 'The Holy Family') is the product of the faith and unique vision of Antoni Gaudi (1852–1926). Still being built and scheduled to be completed in 2026, it was, said the devout Catholic Gaudi, to be 'the last great sanctuary of Christendom'. Its irregular and fantastically intricate style owes something to Art Nouveau, but is impossible to categorize. Its Catholic symbolism is central to the whole vision. It has 18 towers of differing sizes, which represent the 12 Apostles, the four gospel writers, the Virgin Mary and – the tallest – Jesus Christ himself.

Brasilia: The Cathedral of Our Lady of Aparecida was designed by Oscar Niemeyer (b.1907) in the 1950s as part of the new capital of Brazil. A pioneer in the use of reinforced concrete for building, Niemeyer's striking white design is shaped like two hands reaching upward to heaven.

Liverpool: The Metropolitan Cathedral of Christ the King, known locally as 'Paddy's Wigwam', stands on the site allocated to an earlier design by Edwin Lutyens (1869–1944) that would have rivalled Saint Peter's in Rome, but was deemed, in the austerity after World War II, to be too expensive. Frederick Gibberd's (1908–84) radical concrete and glass structure, with a central round tower of stained glass, has become a symbol of Liverpool since its consecration in 1967.

Paris: The Basilica of Sacre Coeur (the Sacred Heart) stands on top of Montmartre, its white stone making it a feature of the city's skyline. Begun in Romano-Byzantine style in the 1870s, its construction was dogged by differences between the secular government of France and the Catholic Church. It was completed in 1914, long after architect Paul Abadie (1812–84) had died.

Yamoussoukro: The Basilica of Our Lady of Peace in the administrative capital of the west African state of Ivory Coast was built at the wish of the country's long-serving president, Felix Houphouet-Boigny (1905–93). It follows closely the design of Saint Peter's in Rome and is reputedly the largest Christian church in the world. Pope John Paul II consecrated it in 1990, but insisted that a hospital be built in its shadow.

The Catholic writer

The term 'Catholic writer' is a popular one, usually employed loosely to describe writers who are also Catholics and who touch on Catholic themes in their books. If strictly interpreted, however, the only ones who can truly claim to be 'Catholic writers' are those whose works receive the Imprimatur – or blessing – of their local bishop. This confirms that there are no errors in matters of faith in the text, and that it is therefore suitable reading for Catholics. However, imprimaturs are usually only sought for books of scholarship or theology.

The English novelist, Graham Greene (1904–91), a convert to the Church in 1926, was often labelled a, if not *the*, Catholic writer. He disliked the term and rejected it. Instead he described his faith as 'doubting my own doubts'. The phrase gives an indication of the themes he explored in his 'Catholic' novels. Those with the most profound exploration of Catholic themes include *Brighton Rock*, *The Heart of the Matter*, *The End of the Affair* and *The Power and the Glory*.

Other 'Catholic writers' include:

Gerard Manley Hopkins (1844–89): Jesuit priest-poet, unpublished in his lifetime, he was a major influence on twentieth-century verse and mixes spiritual insights with acute observations of nature.

G. K. Chesterton (1874–1936): British novelist, journalist and writer of Christian apologetics, he converted to Catholicism as an adult and is best remembered today for his Father Brown detective fiction.

Francois Mauriac (1885–1970): French novelist who was awarded the Nobel Prize for Literature in 1952 'for the deep spiritual insight and artistic intensity' of his novels which are suffused by a sense (often dark) of religion. Sometimes he approached his theme indirectly – as in *Therese Desqueyroux* (1927) – but also tackled issues such as Catholic guilt directly in *Le Mystere Frontenac* (1933).

Morris West (1916–99): The Australian writer trained to be a Christian Brother for 12 years. He returned time and again in his writing to the clash of the sacred and the secular and the existence of evil within organizations set up to do good. His novel *The Shoes of the Fisherman* (1963) predicted the arrival 15 years later of the first Slavic pope.

Andrew Greeley (b.1928): An Irish-American priest, he has written a series of sexually explicit, bestselling romances, which include an undertow of theological debate. They include *The Cardinal Sins* (1981), and in 2004 he tackled the paedophile priest scandal in *Priestly Sin*.

The Da Vinci Code

In 2003, Dan Brown's detective novel, *The Da Vinci Code*, was published and quickly went on to become an international bestseller, with more than 60 million copies sold and translations in 44 languages. A film of the book followed soon afterwards. The plot focuses on the Catholic Church and how it has allegedly covered up certain 'truths' about Jesus Christ – namely that he didn't die on the Cross but married Mary Magdalene and had children with her. It brings into its narrative the extra-canonical gospels, legends of a miraculous Holy Grail, taken to France, and contains a profoundly unflattering portrait of the Catholic organization, Opus Dei, which is portrayed as having great but sinister influence at the heart of Catholicism.

Though the book is fiction, its author insists that all the details included are based on careful research and 'fact'. If taken at this level, it damns Catholicism as a hypocritical, murderous institution and the claims of Christianity as essentially false. Catholic scholars have subsequently challenged Brown's research and sources, and in particular his use of disputed 'evidence' to present an alternative narrative of Christ's life and legacy.

Opus Dei

Opus Dei is an organization of just 87,000 members, founded in Spain in the late 1920s by Father Josemaria Escriva. It was given papal approval in 1950 and was created a personal prelature by Pope John Paul II in 1982 – freeing it from the authority of local bishops.

The core idea of Opus Dei is that sanctity is to be found in the midst of ordinary life. Around 70 per cent of its members live and work in society, and are dedicated to spreading the faith among those they meet. Only 30 per cent are celibate and a smaller proportion are priests. It has a large number of 'associates' who are linked to Opus Dei but are not members of it.

Opus Dei cherishes a traditional view both of Catholicism and social organization. In its residences, for instance, men and women are segregated. It has provoked controversy both inside and outside the Church over a number of its practices including:

- its methods of recruiting students which have been decried by some former members as akin to brainwashing or a cult
- the mortification of the flesh – by whips or spiky bracelets worn on the upper thigh – performed by some members
- its alleged secretiveness, particularly over its finances
- its political links with right-wing regimes, especially that of the dictator Franco in Spain
- the personality of Father Escriva, who was canonized by Pope John Paul II in 2002.

On that occasion the Pope described Escriva as 'among the great witnesses of Christianity', and 'the saint of ordinary life'. He praised Opus Dei for 'its aim [of] the sanctification of one's life, while remaining within the world at one's place of work and profession: to live the Gospel in the world, while living immersed in the world, but in order to transform it, and to redeem it with one's personal love for Christ. This is truly a great ideal, which right from the beginning has anticipated the theology of the lay state of the Second Vatican Council and the post-conciliar period.'

Pope Benedict XVI has praised Father Escriva for correcting the mistaken idea that holiness is reserved to extraordinary people who are completely different from ordinary sinners, and has applauded Opus Dei's 'surprising union of absolute fidelity to the Church's great tradition, to its faith, and unconditional openness to all the challenges of this world, whether in the academic world, in the field of work, or in matters of the economy, etc.'

Other modern movements

In addition to Opus Dei, several other new Catholic movements, all supported enthusiastically by the papacy, have been established to meet the challenges of living a spiritual life in a secular society. Amongst them are:

Communion and Liberation is a movement of lay people in Italy, though it has spread in recent years internationally. It defines its purpose as 'the education to Christian maturity of its adherents and collaboration in the mission of the Church in all the spheres of contemporary life'. Its founder was Father Luigi Giusanni (1922–2005), an Italian priest and schoolteacher. It has no form of membership, but encourages all who are interested to come along to weekly sessions known as 'Schools of Community'.

Focolare, founded in northern Italy in 1943 by Chiara Lubich (1922–2008), has around 90,000 members worldwide, many of whom live in communities and take vows of celibacy. Its name comes from the Italian for 'family fireside' and its principal work is in the promotion of Christian unity.

The Neo-Catechumenate is dedicated to the renewal of the Church adovated by the Second Vatican Council. Founded by Spanish painter and former atheist, Kiko Arguello (b.1939) in 1968, it tries to imitate the early Christian communities in its structures and dynamism. It has a particular interest in making converts from other faiths and numbers 13,500 small communities around the world, often based in parishes.

The **Catholic Charismatic Renewal Movement** has close ties with charismatic movements in the Pentecostal and Evangelical Churches. It lays particular emphasis on vibrant worship, modern music and the role of the Holy Spirit. At charismatic services, the gifts of the Holy Spirit, referred to in the New Testament, are often in evidence, with people 'talking in tongues' (glossolalia – speaking in words that are apparently unintelligible), interpreting (what is being said in tongues), and healing. A development of the late 1960s, it represents another attempt to promote the ideals of the Second Vatican Council and was guided for many years by the prominent Council

Father, Cardinal Leo-Josephus Suenens from Belgium (1904–96). It found particular inspiration in the words of *Lumen Gentium*: 'It is not only through the sacraments and the ministrations of the Church that the Holy Spirit makes holy the people, leads them and enriches them with his virtues... He also distributes special graces among the faithful of every rank. By these gifts he makes them fit and ready to undertake various tasks and offices for the renewal and building up of the Church.'

Conclusion

In meeting the challenge of the modern world, Catholics and their Church have taken many approaches, some of them very different from each other. What unites them is their loyalty to the papacy and their desire to ensure that Catholicism's message reaches even skeptical audiences and all those who could potentially benefit from it.

conclusion

One, Holy, Catholic and Apostolic Church

The 1.2 billion Catholics in the world belong, in theory and in the popular imagination, to a Church that is as wide-ranging in its geographical spread as it is precise and united in its teachings. Again, in theory, there is little room for regional variations on the theme of what is laid down in a self-avowedly hierarchical and non-democratic organization. The Pope, based in the Vatican, has a unique and, according to Catholic doctrine, occasionally infallible authority to teach, based on scripture and the traditions of the Church. There should be, as Catholics state in the Creed, just 'One, Holy, Catholic and Apostolic Church' – as indeed there is.

One of the aspects of being a member of the Catholic Church is that sense of being part of something so much bigger than national or even continental boundaries. Catholicism appears to have managed to distil down in its core beliefs something that has a power to unite humankind around the globe. Attend a Mass in Addis Ababa, the Amazon basin or Aldershot and in the Catholic liturgy there is a familiarity that conveys that participants are part of a global family.

Yet, it is a familiarity that cannot disguise that there are huge economic, political and social differences between the world's Catholics. These are inevitable in such a far-flung organization that stretches from the wealthy capitals of the developed world to the favelas of South America and the shanty towns of Africa, from presidents, prime ministers and kings to the most needy and marginalized on the planet.

As a consequence, there are differences in emphasis as to what it means to be a Catholic between individual believers and between believers in individual societies, which each have their own priorities, history, culture, customs and baggage. English Catholics, for instance, remain in some way shaped by the experience of their Church being suppressed for almost 300 years following the Reformation.

More generally, there remains an undeniable gap between the ideals that the Church teaches and the reality of many Catholics' lives. Not every Catholic follows to the letter every teaching of the Church. The areas of divergence from those teachings, and the degree, will be wide-ranging and, sometimes, will appear to follow no obvious logic. So those who, for instance, prefer a 'traditional' Latin liturgy will often also be the ones pushing for the Church to take a more 'progressive' stance on social justice. And those who embrace a 'modern' free style of worship will, sometimes, be the ones who are defiantly 'un-modern' in their stance on matters of personal morality.

The reason for such disparity comes down in part to economics and politics – what is possible and desirable in different societies around the world – and in part to personal temperament and conscience. Catholics live their lives in the context of radically different societies that shape the daily reality of their faith.

Yet for all that, at core, there continues to be, after 2000 years, a template of beliefs and a liturgy at the heart of global Catholicism that unites more than it divides. And, as the symbol of that unity, the Pope, in the Vatican and on his travels, remains the visible sign of the Catholic Church.

glossary

Angelus A short, traditional set of prayers, performed several times daily, to remind Catholics of Jesus' incarnation on earth as both human and divine.

Apocrypha The sacred books that have not been included by the Church in either the Old or New Testaments.

Apostolic Succession The belief in Catholicism that Jesus chose Saint Peter from amongst his Apostles to be the first leader and Pope of his church on earth, and that each Pope thereafter is linked via Peter to Christ.

Beatification When the Church declares someone who has died to be 'Blessed'. This is done after an investigation of their life and is only awarded if that life is shown to have been one of exceptional faith. A further requirement is that the Church is satisfied that one miraculous cure has resulted from the intercession of that individual from beyond the grave. Beatification is a step on the path to canonisation

Benediction A short prayer for divine help, often part of a service.

Canonization When the Church declares someone a saint. The qualifications are the same as in the case of beatification, but with one major difference. It requires proof of two miracles.

Catechism A rule book for Catholics.

Council of Trent The key meeting, held intermittently in the Italian city of the same name between 1545 and 1563, when the Catholic Church formulated its response to the Reformation.

Charism From the Greek for grace, the influence of the divine experienced as a gift within individuals.

Curia The bureaucracy that serves the popes in Rome.

Divine Office A structure of prayers and readings to cover the whole day.

The Enlightenment An eighteenth century philosophical movement in Western Europe which rejected religious pessimism as to the sinfulness of humankind and preached instead optimism and the power of each human being to reach their potential on earth.

Eucharist One of the seven sacraments, also known as Holy Communion

Extreme Unction Meaning 'final anointing' and a traditional phrase for the sacrament given to those believed to be nearing death.

Gentile In the early Christian Church, and in the New Testament, gentile is a phrase used to describe non-Jews.

Holy See Another phrase to describe the Vatican, derived from a phrase used in the enthronement ceremony of popes.

Homily A commentary on scripture, usually given during the mass.

Iconoclasm The destruction of religious icons, seen within the Orthodox Church in eighth and ninth century.

Imprimatur The formal approval of the local bishop, given to a book or document produced by a priest or religious under his authority, and an indication that what is said or written fits with the teachings of the Catholic Church.

Indulgences The full or partial remission of punishments or penances to be done in this life for sins committed against church teaching and confessed to a priest.

Judaism The faith and beliefs of Jews.

Liturgy The form of words and music used by the Church for its services.

Magisterium The teaching authority of the church, usually vested in the person of the Pope.

Mass The celebration of the Eucharist.

Mendicant From the Latin to beg, this refers to monks and religious who rely exclusively on charity to survive.

Ostpolitik The policy of the Vatican, in the wake of the Second World War, of entering into constructive dialogue with communist regimes in eastern Europe which rejected religion.

Papacy The noun used to describe the office of the popes.

Patriarchate Refers to the ecclesiastical authority of patriarchs, senior figures in the early Church who rivalled the bishops of Rome.

Rosary A Catholic ritual, using beads, where a strict formula of prayers is repeated while individuals reflect on events in the life of the Virgin Mary

Sacred Rota One of the highest appeal courts in the Catholic Church's system of Church (or Canon) Law

Simony The sin of paying for offices or positions in the hierarchy of the church, named after Simon Magus, who appears in the Acts of the Apostles (8:18-24). Simon Magus offers the disciples, Peter and John, payment if anyone he placed his hands on would then receive the power of the Holy Spirit

Solemnities A principal holy day in the church's calendar

Synod A church meeting, often of bishops and cardinals

Transubstantiation The Catholic belief that Jesus' body and blood are present in the bread and wine at Holy Communion in more than a purely symbolic way

Trinitarian Anything to do with the Holy Trinity, the three persons in one God: Father, Son and Holy Spirit

Trinity The Christian belief that there are three persons in one God: God the Father, God the Son (Jesus), and God the Holy Spirit.

Ultramontanism The belief that the Pope's powers override those of any local secular or church figure. It literally means 'over the mountains' and refers to attempts to make the Pope's word as important in faraway countries as it was in Rome.

taking it further

Websites

The Catholic Agency to Support Evangelization (CASE) offers materials for those interested in Catholicism – www.caseresources.org.uk – or write to them c/o 39 Eccleston Square, London SW1V 1BX. It also operates the Catholic Enquiry Centre which can be reached via www.life4seekers.co.uk

Face to face

The most direct route is to attend your local Catholic Church and/or to make contact with your local priest. The Church runs a series of programmes in each parish and diocese for those interested in exploring the Catholic faith. If you feel nervous of face-to-face contact, there will be a range of booklets at the back of the Church, along with copies of the vibrant national Catholic press.

Further reading

On Catholics

Gilley, S. (1990) *Newman and His Age*, DLT
Sewell, D. (2001) *Catholics: Britain's Largest Minority*, Viking
Maddocks, F. (2001) *Hildegard of Bingen*, Hodder Headline
Purves, L. (1998) *Holy Smoke*, Hodder & Stoughton
Stanford, P. (ed.) (2005) *Why I Am Still A Catholic*, Continuum
Wills, G. (1999) *Saint Augustine*, Weidenfeld

On Church history

Green, T. (2007) *Inquisition*, Macmillan
Kung, H. (2001) *The Catholic Church: A Short History*, Weidenfeld

Longley, C. (1999) *The Worlock Archive*, Chapman

Noel, G. (1994) *Anatomy of the Catholic Church*, Michael Russell

Stourton, E. (1998) *Absolute Truth: The Catholic Church in the World Today*, Viking

Wright, J. (2004) *The Jesuits*, HarperCollins

On Women religious

McNamara, J. A. K. (1996) *Sisters in Arms: Catholic Nuns Through Two Millennia*, Harvard

Sebba, A. (1997) Mother Teresa: Beyond The Image, Weidenfeld

On Pope John Paul II

Pope John Paul II (1994) *Crossing The Threshold of Hope*, Cape

Pope John Paul II (2004) *Rise, Let Us Be On Our Way*, Cape

Pope John Paul II (2005) *Memory and Identity: Personal Reflections*, Weidenfeld

O'Connor, G. (2005) *Universal Father*, Bloomsbury

Stourton, E. (2006) *John Paul II: Man of History*, Hodder Headline

On Opus Dei

Allen, J. L. (2005) *Opus Dei: Secrets and Power Inside the Catholic Church*, Allen Lane

On Papacy

Allen, J. L. (2000) *Cardinal Ratzinger*, Continuum

Duffy, E. (1997) *Saints and Sinners: A History of the Popes*, Yale

Shortt, R. (2005) *Benedict XVI*, Hodder & Stoughton

On pilgrimage

Seward. D. (1993) *The Dancing Sun: Journeys to The Miracle Shrines*, Fount

Toibin, C. (1994) *The Signs of the Cross: Travels in Catholic Europe*, J Cape

On Pius XII's wartime record

Cornwell, J. (1997) *Hitler's Pope*, Viking

Goldhagen, J. (2002) *A Moral Reckoning*, Little Brown

On spirituality

Torkington, D. (1997) *Inner Life: A Fellow Traveller's Guide to Prayer*, DLT

On suffering

Craig. M. (1979) *Blessings*, Hodder & Stoughton

On women priests

Byrne, L. (1994) *Woman At The Altar: The Ordination of Women in the Roman Catholic Church*, Continuum
Torjesen, K. J. (1993) *When Women Were Priests*, HarperSan Francisco

index